MW00830071

Quarter-Mile
MUSTANGS

Doug Boyce

CarTech®

THE HISTORY OF
Ford's Pony Car at the Drag Strip 1964½–1978

CarTech®

CarTech®, Inc.
6118 Main Street
North Branch, MN 55056
Phone: 651-277-1200 or 800-551-4754
Fax: 651-277-1203
www.cartechbooks.com

© 2022 by Doug Boyce

All rights reserved. No part of this publication may be reproduced or utilized in any form or by any means, electronic or mechanical, including photocopying, recording, or by any information storage and retrieval system, without prior permission from the Publisher. All text, photographs, and artwork are the property of the Author unless otherwise noted or credited.

The information in this work is true and complete to the best of our knowledge. However, all information is presented without any guarantee on the part of the Author or Publisher, who also disclaim any liability incurred in connection with the use of the information and any implied warranties of merchantability or fitness for a particular purpose. Readers are responsible for taking suitable and appropriate safety measures when performing any of the operations or activities described in this work.

All trademarks, trade names, model names and numbers, and other product designations referred to herein are the property of their respective owners and are used solely for identification purposes. This work is a publication of CarTech, Inc., and has not been licensed, approved, sponsored, or endorsed by any other person or entity. The Publisher is not associated with any product, service, or vendor mentioned in this book, and does not endorse the products or services of any vendor mentioned in this book.

Edit by Wes Eisenschenk
Layout by Connie DeFlorin

ISBN 978-1-61325-598-8
Item No. CT680

Library of Congress Cataloging-in-Publication Data Available

Written, edited, and designed in the U.S.A.
Printed in China
10 9 8 7 6 5 4 3 2 1

CarTech books may be purchased at a discounted rate in bulk for resale, events, corporate gifts, or educational purposes. Special editions may also be created to specification. For details, contact Special Sales at 6118 Main Street, North Branch, MN 55056 or by email at sales@cartechbooks.com.

PUBLISHER'S NOTE: In reporting history, the images required to tell the tale will vary greatly in quality, especially by modern photographic standards. While some images in this volume are not up to those digital standards, we have included them, as we feel they are an important element in telling the story.

DISTRIBUTION BY:

Europe
PGUK
63 Hatton Garden
London EC1N 8LE, England
Phone: 020 7061 1980 • Fax: 020 7242 3725
www.pguk.co.uk

Australia
Renniks Publications Ltd.
3/37-39 Green Street
Banksmeadow, NSW 2109, Australia
Phone: 2 9695 7055 • Fax: 2 9695 7355
www.renniks.com

Canada
Login Canada
300 Saulteaux Crescent
Winnipeg, MB, R3J 3T2 Canada
Phone: 800 665 1148 • Fax: 800 665 0103
www.lb.ca

TABLE OF CONTENTS

Introduction 6

Chapter 1: 1964–1966: New Kid on the Block 8
Chapter 2: 1967–1968 Competition Breeds Success 28
Chapter 3: 1969–1970 Meet the New Boss 46
Chapter 4: 1971–1973: New Styling,
                Same Go-Fast Goodness 71
Chapter 5: 1974–1978: It's a Mustang Too 99

Epilogue 141

INTRODUCTION

The Mustang has been one of the greatest automotive success stories of all time. Its impact has been felt near and far. In the sport of drag racing, the Mustang played a significant role in the evolution of the Funny Car and has been a dominant force in both the Stock and Super Stock categories. To tell the story of the Mustang's drag racing history, you need to go back to 1961, when Ford's interest in the sport first took hold.

The year 1961 was the beginning of the factory wars between Detroit's Big Three: GM, Ford, and Chrysler. Each manufacturer set out to win the hearts (and wallets) of the war babies, who were now coming of age. "Race on Sunday and Sell on Monday" was the catch phrase coined by Bob Tasca Sr. and adopted by Detroit's Big Three. Specially prepared cars battled it out in Super Stock, as 390-powered Galaxies butted heads with 409 Chevys, 389 Pontiacs, and 413 Mopars. Taking a cue from the backyard builder, the biggest engine in the lightest package, Detroit upped the ante for 1962 by releasing a limited run of cars that featured lightweight fiberglass or aluminum panels. Showing that it meant business, Ford stretched the 390 out to 406 ci.

The battles escalated in 1963. Ford's lightweight 406-ci Galaxies (prepared by Les Ritchey, Dick Brannan, and Bill Lawton) were more than holding their own against the 426 Max Wedge Mopars, 427 Impalas, and 421-ci "Swiss cheese" Pontiacs. After 1963, Ford and Chrysler were the only two left in the game. GM, fearing government intervention, fell back on the 1957 AMA ban on participating in organized motorsports and pulled the plug on all racing activity.

In 1964, Ford introduced the 427 Thunderbolt, a limited run of Super Stock Fairlanes that were built to topple the Plymouths and Dodges that were lighter by design and now powered by the newly introduced 426 Hemi. The Thunderbolt accomplished what it set out to do; Gas Ronda won Super Stock at the Winternationals, and Butch Leal followed by winning Super Stock at Indy.

Chrysler introduced its altered wheelbase A/Factory Experimental cars in 1964, and there was no way Ford was going to sit on its laurels. When the Mustang was released in April 1964, Ford found its new performance leader.

The sporty looking Mustang was an instant hit with the buying public. First-year sales saw more than 400,000 units pass through showroom doors. The Mustang helped usher in a whole new market of car, the pony car, and it took another three years before Chrysler and GM had a car to compete with it.

To counter Chrysler's Hemi, Ford spent 90 days in mid-1965 and came up with the single overhead cam (SOHC) 427, and what better platform than the Mustang to mount it? Ford's Drag Council members each received an SOHC 427-powered Mustang and the cars sent the Hemi Mopars packing. At the Nationals, Gas Ronda's SOHC Mustang defeated the similar car of Les Ritchey in the A/FX class final.

In 1966, Ford had Holman-Moody-Stroppe build several altered wheelbase Mustangs that featured a tube chassis and fiberglass body. It was the birth of the Funny Car, and the Mustang, with its nitro-inhaling SOHC 427, was right in the thick of the action. Over the next couple of years, the Mustang pulled in wins from leaders such as Tommy Grove, Bob Tasca, and Gas Ronda. Ronda's long-nose Mustang was the first Exhibition Stocker to run an 8-second ET.

For 1968, Ford listened to the cries for a potent street-performing variant for the masses and introduced the 428 Cobra Jet Mustang. The company put its Drag Council members in Mustangs for the 1968 Winternationals and saw member Al Joniec win Super Stock Eliminator. Produced between the years 1968 and 1970, no other Mustang has provided Ford with more class wins and records. For decades, these cars have all but owned their respective Stock and Super Stock classes.

The 351 Cleveland, with its smooth flowing ports and beautifully canted valves, was introduced in 1969 and was the scourge of 1970s Pro Stock. Many-a-Mustang won national events and the world title in 1977 when placed in the downsized Mustang II. In spite of the NHRA's attempt to slow down the Fords with extra weight, Bob Glidden, Don Nicholson, and Gapp & Roush all earned wins with the Mustang.

When it came to match racing these door cars,

the big-inch Mustang IIs paved the way right into the 7-second zone. Dyno Don was the first, and close behind was Rickie Smith, whose Mustang II won several IHRA championships into the 1980s. Adding to the list were wins by Harold Denton and Ronnie Sox, who propelled Fox Body Mustangs into the winner's circle.

Celebrating the release of the original Cobra Jet Mustang 40 years prior, in 2008 Ford unleashed 50 Factory Stock Cobra Jet Mustangs. To create this factory drag car, Ford Performance took its most powerful engine (a 425-hp supercharged dual-overhead-cam [DOHC] 5.4L) and dropped it into a stripped-down, race-ready Mustang.

Enthusiast Brent Hajek purchased the first 10 produced and prepared four of them to race at the 2009 Win-ternationals. In a final that could have only been written in the stars, veteran racer John Calvert, driving the Al Joniec, Rice Holman AA/Stock tribute Mustang won the category final.

As of this writing, the Factory Stock Showdown Mustangs continue to be a dominant force. Bill and Drew Skillman have their supercharged Factory Mustangs running low 7.70 times. Chris Holbrook, following in his dad's footsteps, was the points leader in 2020. However, harking back to the 1970s, the Mustangs are once again being hampered by rules. What's the old saying? The more things change, the more they stay the same.

We're 58 years beyond the birth of the Mustang, and it continues to be a leader in the sport. No doubt the success stories will continue well into the foreseeable future.

(Photo Courtesy David Newhardt/Mecum Auctions)

CHAPTER 1

1964-1966

NEW KID ON THE BLOCK

The Mustang made its debut on April 17, 1964, and though it may be an old cliché to say, the automotive world has never been the same. Riding on a 108-inch wheelbase, the Mustang's long hood, short deck design was single-handedly responsible for creating a whole new class of car: the pony car.

Initially, Mustang buyers were limited to coupes and convertibles before a fastback was added in September as a 1965 model. By the end of the 1965 model year, Ford had sold approximately 680,000 Mustangs. To keep production costs down, Ford incorporated many Falcon underpinnings. With a V-8 under the hood (either a 260- or a 289-ci), the Mustang weighed right around 3,000 pounds. It was perfect for those who planned on drag racing.

So popular was the new Mustang that demand created an instant backlog. Additional pressure was added when the car was chosen for the 1964 Indianapolis 500. There were three Holman-Moody-prepared pace car convertibles produced, and an additional 30 convertibles and approximately 190 replicas were provided for official use. (Photo Courtesy James Smart)

1964-1965: Making Plans

From a performance perspective, 1964 was a phenomenal year for Ford. It had the lightweight, 427-equipped Galaxies that were killing the competition in Stock, it had Super Stock covered with the 427-equipped Fairlane Thunderbolt, and it had just introduced the new performance leader in the Mustang. Lightweight and compact, drag racers immediately took to the car. The top engine option was the Hi-Po 271-hp 289, but the gearheads had other ideas. If the 427 could fit in a Fairlane... Hmmm.

TOP LEFT: *This image is from October 6, 1962. The Mustang 1 experimental concept car was more like a GT-40 than a production Mustang, but it had to start somewhere. The actual production Mustang was built on the Falcon platform. (Photo Courtesy Randy Hernandez)*

The First A/FX Mustang

Ron Pellegrini saw further potential in the Mustang, and with full support from his boss at Hawkinson Ford in Oaklawn, Illinois, he shoehorned a hi-rise 427 between the frame rails of a newly released coupe. Hawkinson had taken delivery of three 427-ci Thunderbolts in 1964: two 4-speed cars and one automatic). The automatic transmission–equipped car was sold off, and one of the 4-speed cars became the Hawkinson Ford–sponsored *Thunder Hawk* driven by Pellegrini. Ron stated that he saw a lot of changes coming from the other manufacturers (Chrysler—because GM was out of racing) and knew the Thunderbolt wasn't going to be competitive for very

Mustangs showed up early on the nation's drag strips. One of the first was the C/MP 1965 ragtop belonging to Michigan's "Snooks" Inglett. Snooks is shown in action at the 1965 NHRA Springnationals, where mid-12-second ETs made the program.

Shelby Has More

For the performance-minded Mustang buyer, the 271-hp 289 was the top choice through 1966. If buyers wanted more, there was always the 306-hp Shelby Mustang that was introduced in 1965. The 289's 271 hp came at 6,000 rpm and, in contrast to the standard production 289s (Challenger and Challenger Special), it carried stronger connecting rods with 3/8-inch bolts, thicker main bearing caps, a solid-lift cam, screw-in rocker-arm studs, machined valve-spring seats, a 600-cfm Autolite carburetor, dual-point distributor, and free-flowing exhaust.

Ford only offered a four-month warranty on the high-performance engine, as opposed to its standard two-year warranty. Obviously, Ford had no doubt what the buyer had in mind when ordering the Hi-Po engine. *MotorTrend* magazine helped the reader see the potential. It tested a 271-hp 2+2 equipped with a 4-speed transmission and recorded a quarter-mile time of 15.7 at 89 mph.

Mel Burns Ford in Long Beach jumped on the high-performance sales bandwagon in 1965 and campaigned this Les Ritchey-prepped Shelby. Don McCain drove the car to an AHRA record time of 12.50 at 112.97 mph, using a Weber-equipped 289. Early in 1966, the Mustang received a single 4-barrel Gurney-Weslake 535-hp 305-ci engine and ran C/MSP. (Photo Courtesy Forrest Bond)

The Shelby Mustangs were regulated to the Sports Production classes, as modifications kept them out of Stock. Here, Russell Haslage from Glendora, California, in his George May Ford-sponsored Shelby was having his fun at Indy running B/SP. (Photo Courtesy Forrest Bond)

The Quarter Horse *cut the quarter-mile in 10.90 at 130 mph. The car ran in NHRA A/FX class, which debuted in 1962. Ron Pellegrini had hopes of seeing his 427 creation produced in limited numbers by Ford. (Photo Courtesy Charles Morris)*

long. It didn't take much to convince Hawkinson, and Hawkinson gave Ron the green light to pull the running gear from the second 4-speed Thunderbolt and transplant it into the Mustang.

Before completing the transplant, Ron opened up the firewall of the Mustang to set the 427 back farther in the chassis. In A/FX competition, the smaller, lighter Mustang proved to be unbeatable, running high-10-second times and winning its class at Cordova's World Championship drags and the Meet of Champions at U.S. 30 Dragway.

In the fall of 1964, Ford approached Ron about building a string of 100 similarly equipped Mustangs. He took his car to Ford's proving grounds in Michigan for testing and felt the tests were successful. However, the collaboration never got off the ground.

Seeing how quickly things were evolving, Ford backed out, figuring the cars would be obsolete by the time they hit the track. Ron, trying to get ahead of the quickly changing landscape, then approached Ford with the idea of building a supercharged, tube chassis, fiberglass Mustang. Ford passed on the idea, somehow figuring the cars wouldn't work. Of course, Mercury proved Ford wrong when it released the flip-up Comets in 1966.

Ron never doubted the idea of a fiberglass Mustang, and with booked match race dates in hand, it was time to get busy making what he would call his Super Mustang. With time being of the essence, he purchased the Fuel roadster of Dennison, Arlansky, and Knox and placed one of his Fiberglass Ltd. Mustang bodies on it.

Working with a 97-inch-wheelbase chassis, Ron had to slice the body through the middle to shorten it. Going against better judgment, Pellegrini ran with a blown Chrysler Hemi, which propelled the Mustang into the 8.80s at 160 mph. Having a tube chassis, fiberglass body, and a blown engine on nitro, Ron considered the Mustang to be the first true Funny Car.

Factory Experimental

The Factory Experimental category was created in 1962. From the get-go it was used by Detroit's Big Three as a place to wage war. Although bodies had to be stock in appearance, rules did allow for use of lightweight panels of fiberglass or aluminum. Chassis were lightened, and thin-gauge glass or Plexiglas windows were usually incorporated.

Regarding the drivetrain, pretty much anything went, as long as it carried a factory part number. Classes ran A through C and were determined by a weight-to-cubic inch factor. The category was initially dominated by lightweight Galaxies, Corvette-powered Chevy IIs, and 421-powered Pontiac Tempests. The battles raged on, and in 1965, things escalated to the point where Ford had no choice but to up its game to combat Chrysler's "funny cars."

In stepped the SOHC-powered Mustang. The category ran through 1966 before disappearing and was replaced by Experimental Stock.

Phil Bonner, also known as "Daddy Warbucks," was always a fan favorite. He received one of the first altered wheelbase 1965 Mustangs and is shown burning it through the rosin at Houston Raceway. (Photo Courtesy Forrest Bond)

Ford Calls on Dearborn Steel Tubing

Ford's rejection of Pellegrini's Mustang may have had more to do with the fact that it had a better idea in the wings. In July 1965, Andy Hotton's Dearborn Steel Tubing (DST) was commissioned to build a 427-equipped Mustang. The car would be similar to Pellegrini's (minus the setback engine). According to Ford's Bill Holbrook, a white Mustang (VIN 5F07F100028) was shipped from the Dearborn assembly plant to DST for modifications to the shock towers to fit the 427. The Mustang was then sent to Ford's Experimental Vehicles garage for drag racing development. It was fitted with a 9-inch rear end that carried 4.86 gears, a Thunderbolt driveshaft, and 66-inch-long traction bars that connected the rear end to the front sub-frame.

Kenny Salter built the hi-rise engine that was backed by a Toploader. All of the essentials, including headers and mounts, were fabricated. Bringing the weight down to 3,200 pounds were fiberglass parts (including fenders, the hood, and doors) and Plexiglas side windows. Initial runs by driver Len Ritcher took place at Detroit Dragway, where the Mustang recorded an 11.50 at 123 mph. The Mustang appeared at the NHRA Nationals on Labor Day weekend, but mechanical gremlins kept it on the side-lines. The Mustang was passed on to Salter, and he subsequently wrecked it.

Plans in 1964 called for a run of 50 427 hi-rise Mustangs to be built to run NHRA Super Stock. But when NASCAR refused to accept the exotic SOHC 427, it allowed Ford to rethink its initial plans. Out was the Super Stock hi-rise Mustang, and in was the SOHC A/FX Mustang.

Dearborn Steel Tubing built two initial SOHC mule Mustangs while Holman-Moody in Charlotte, North Carolina, built 10 more cars in December. Eight cars went to Drag Council members while one was retained by Holman-Moody and the other went to Ford. To fit the Cammer within the tight confines of the Mustang engine bay, the coil-spring suspension and shock towers were swapped out and replaced with an unorthodox twisted leaf spring suspension. The design featured a single leaf per side that had one end bolted to the lower control arm and the other end bolted to the radiator support member. The setup worked in a similar fashion to a torsion bar suspension. It also helped align the suspension and allowed for the removal of the strut rods.

Further room was found within the engine bay by replacing the steering box with an Australian Falcon box that allowed for mounting on the outer side of the left frame rail. To help keep the weight down (the Cammer

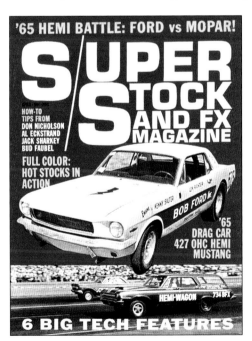

Len Ritcher drove the experimental Hemi Hunter *Mustang*, which was a 427 hi-rise coupe built in July 1964 by Dearborn Steel Tubing. When Len received his SOHC Mustang, this one was passed on to Ken Salter.

Unwilling to take a backseat to the Mopars in A/FX, Ford unleashed the 427 Mustang. The competition didn't have a chance. This is one of the two mule cars built by Dearborn Steel Tubing in July 1964 and is powered by a hi-rise 427. (Photo Courtesy Dick Brannan)

December 1964 saw Dick Brannan testing the Mustang A/FX test mule at Pomona. Dick had joined Ford in 1962 when the company hired him as drag racing coordinator. (Photo Courtesy Dick Brannan)

Philadelphia-based Al Joniec and his Wedge-head 427 A/FX Mustang had no problem keeping up with the SOHC 427 Mustangs. Ten-second ETs and wheels-in-the-air launches made Al's Mustang a fan favorite. In short order, a Cammer was swapped in. (Photo Courtesy Al Joniec)

weighs 120 pounds more than the 427 Wedge), the doors, fenders, hood, and front bumper were formed using fiberglass.

Plexiglas windows were added, and frivolous items, such as a radio, wipers, heater, and insulation were never added as the cars rolled down the assembly line. Filling the trunk and helping balance the weight was a hefty truck battery. Rounding out the drivetrain was a mandatory 4-speed and a 9-inch rear supported by adjustable ladder bars. With safety in mind, a roll bar, safety harness, and disc brakes were all standard equipment.

Holman-Moody-Stroppe

No other names seem to grab more attention in Ford circles than Holman-Moody-Stroppe. Here's a brief history on how the trio came to be household names.

Holman went to work for Bill Stroppe in 1952. Stroppe had established a relationship with Ford in 1947 after defeating Ford-sponsored teams at the Henry Ford Memorial Regatta boat race. Holman worked for him through 1956 before Ford hired him away. Moody, a racer himself, hooked up with Holman in 1957 and won the first two Grand National races of the season.

When Ford signed the original AMA ban in 1957 and pulled out of racing, Holman and Moody pooled their resources and purchased Ford's Charlotte operations. In 1958, they opened a shop in North Carolina where they became the winningest team in NASCAR history by racking up 92 wins and 2 championships. In 1959, Ford, slowly slipping back into racing, came knocking. The pair were provided 10 assembly-line Thunderbirds to prep for NASCAR competition.

In 1965, Holman and Moody bought out Bill Stroppe and his Long Beach, California, operation. The shop became famous for building and preparing a countless number of Ford-Mercury race cars. In 1965, the company was contracted by Ford to build SOHC-powered A/FX Mercury Comets and Mustangs.

John Holman (left), Ralph Moody (middle), and Bill Stroppe (right) have been building winning Fords since the mid-1950s and have left their names in all forms of motorsport, including drag racing. (Photos Courtesy Lou Hart and Larry Minor)

The 1965 NHRA Winternationals

Five of the A/FX Mustangs were ready in time to make their debut at the NHRA Winternationals on February 7. Drag Council members in attendance were Gas Ronda, Len Ritcher, Bill Lawton, Phil Bonner, and Dick Brannan. The three remaining member cars for Al Joniec, Clester Andrews, and Les Ritchey initially received Wedge engines due to the fact that at this early stage, the Cammer was still in short supply.

The Winternationals Mustangs were lumped into Factory Stock and competed against four similarly equipped Comets and four Mopars. At the end of the first round of eliminations, four Mustangs remained (Brannan fell to breakage). In the semifinals, Lawton defeated the Plymouth of Tommy Grove, while Ritcher defeated the SOHC-powered Comet of George DeLorean but twisted an axle in the process, which put him out of commission. This left Lawton in the Tasca Mustang to single with a 10.91 at 128.20 mph for the Factory Stock title.

At the inaugural NHRA Springnationals, Lawton was runner-up to the Plymouth of Ronnie Sox. At the Super Stock Nationals, today referred to as drag racing's Woodstock, Lawton defeated the Dodge of Melvin Yow in the 3,200-pound class final.

It was a yearlong battle in the Factory Experimental classes among the Fords, Comets, and Chrysler cars. Factory Experimental rules in 1965 dictated that cars and engines had to be of the current year. Having backed out of racing in 1963, this left GM out in the cold. Factory Experimental rules also stated that the axle could be relocated 2 percent of the original stock location, which was a little something that Chrysler had been practicing since 1964. Come 1965, Chrysler went all out, handing 6 Coronets and 5 Belvederes to Amblewagon in Troy, Michigan, who shifted the front suspension forward 10 inches and the rear, 15 inches. When it came to racing these new-fangled funny cars, Ford had no interest.

A memo released by Leo Beebe, a Ford special vehicle manager, read, ". . . all Ford Mustang A/FX cars have been built according to safety standards and specs of NHRA. We have asked our A/FX drivers (including Mercury) not to compete against cars that do not conform to these specs."

Ford Drag Council Boss Dick Brannan had different feelings.

Gas Ronda ran two different Holman-Moody-built SOHC A/FX Mustangs in 1965, having crashed his first one. One of 10 built, the Mustang dominated, won the AHRA World Finals, and set both ends of the AHRA class record with an ET of 10.43 at 134.73 mph.

The year 1965 proved to be great for Tasca, beginning with a win at the Winternationals. After a runner-up finish at the inaugural NHRA Springnationals in June, driver Bill Lawton was a winner at the Super Stock Nationals, defeating the altered wheelbase Dodge of Cecil Yother in the 3,200-pound class. (Photo Courtesy Bob McClurg)

Ronda's Mustang, like all other factory A/FX Mustangs, retained it showroom interior. Add-ons included the necessary gauges, an aftermarket shifter, a harness, and a roll cage. (Photo Courtesy Zach Straits)

A Change of Plans

With Chrysler seemingly upping the game weekly (adding injectors, alcohol, and then nitromethane), Dick and his boss, Charlie Gray, couldn't sit back. They sent two Mustangs down to Holman-Moody in April for a reworking. Each Mustang had the wheelbase altered 4 inches by moving both the front and rear suspension forward. One car was built with an automatic, while the car that Dick planned on campaigning received a 4-speed. The test car received injectors and nitro, which saw speeds increase into the 150 range. Stability issues at speed led to Dick crashing the test car. The incident sidelined him with four compression fractures to four lower vertebrae. It was at this point that the decision was made for the next batch of Mustangs to have an extended wheelbase.

Dick Brannan puts the heavily modified test mule through its paces. The car was wrecked in a high-speed crash that left Dick with serious injuries. (Photo Courtesy Charles Morris)

A broken axle at the 1965 Winternationals kept Len Ritcher from an A/FX final-round appearance against Tasca's Mustang. Here, at Indy, he lost to Ronda and Ritchey, who battled for class final. Len went back to testing cars for Ford at the end of the season, and the Mustang passed on to Jerry Harvey. (Photo Courtesy Forrest Bond)

The B/Altered class was an odd place to find match race cars, such as Dick Brannan's Mustang and Dyno Don's Comet, but at the Nationals on Labor Day weekend, it was where the NHRA felt that they were best suited. Dick defeated Dyno here in class before losing the final to Jack Ditmar's Lil Screamer due to a blown head gasket. During the previous weekend, Dick won Mr. Stock Eliminator at the AHRA Nationals, where he recorded 10.0 ETs. (Photo Courtesy Forrest Bond)

At the NHRA Nationals in 1965, the A/FX class final boiled down to the SOHC Mustangs of Les Ritchey and Gas Ronda. It was a close one, with Les taking the win on a slight holeshot, recording an ET of 10.67 to a 10.63. Les's Performance Associates Mustang ran Weber carburetors. (Photo Courtesy Forrest Bond)

Brannan debuted the 4-speed Mustang, labeled with the name *Bronco* at the AHRA Summernationals and won the meet, defeating Gas Ronda in the final and recording 10.0 times. At the preceding NHRA Nationals, where the *Bronco* was forced to run B/Altered, Dick set low ET in his class and made it to the final round, where a blown head gasket saw him lose out to Jack Ditmars's *Lil Screamer II*. With the success of the *Bronco*, Ford gave the green light to build a new batch of Mustangs for 1966.

Ed Terry initially ran his Weber-carbureted 289 Mustang in B/FX. The class proved to be a little too crowded with Fords, so he made the switch to C/Gas. Tommy Grove was the brains behind the build, which saw the car win class at the 1966 NHRA Winternationals with an ET of 11.78 at 118.11 mph. (Photo Courtesy Charles Morris)

It's a tight squeeze—even with the shock towers out of the way. Les toyed with the Weber carburetors on the Cammer before eventually returning to twin Holleys. (Photo Courtesy Charles Morris)

Ed Terry takes pride in his winning Weber-carbureted 289. It was assembled by Tommy Grove, who figured out that to build a winning small-block Ford, you couldn't build it like you would build a Chevy. (Photo Courtesy Charles Morris)

Fans and track promoters loved the Batman theme that Al Joniec carried on his Mustang. Built by Holman-Moody, Al's Mustang briefly ran with a Wedge until a Cammer became available. The Mustang later received the stretched nose treatment after it was damaged when it ran off the end of New York National Speedway. (Photo Courtesy Michael Pottie)

And Then There's Ron

Specially prepared Mustangs were showing up in numerous categories. Garnishing attention and racking up the wins were Mustang drivers including Bill Ireland, Darrell Droke, Paul Norris, and Ron Vansteenis, who may not have gotten their share of publicity.

Now, you may have heard of Darrell Droke and Paul Norris, but Ron Vanteenis—probably not. Ron was one of many campaigning a Mustang in Stock Eliminator. Ron had the pleasure of purchasing the first Mustang sold in Albuquerque, New Mexico. It was the only Mustang the dealer had in stock, and within a couple days of purchasing the car, Ron was asked to return it. The demand for Mustangs was so great that the dealership couldn't get its hands on another one and needed to borrow Ron's to showcase the model.

Equipped with a 170-ci 6-cylinder engine and a 3-speed manual transmission, Ron's Mustang was nothing fancy. He increased the output by opening up the engine 0.030 and adding a split header. Ron took it to the drags, where the combo ran in M/S. He made it to the 1965 Winternationals, flat-towing the Mustang behind his father's 1960 Pontiac.

After ingesting some bad gas in Barstow, California, the Pontiac melted a piston.

"We were bellowing black smoke and were stopped by the California Highway Patrol, who suggested we unhook the Mustang to ease the load on the Pontiac and drive the car," Ron said. "I fired up the Mustang with its open exhaust, and the officer just shook his head. He escorted us into Riverside with my wife driving the bellowing Pontiac with our five-month-old baby onboard, and me in the Mustang."

A fruitless trip, Ron was defeated in the class final by the Oldsmobile of Keith Berg. As little consolation, Keith was later disqualified upon teardown.

Way down in L/Stock, Ron Vansteenis managed to squeeze out times in the 15.60s from his 6-cylinder Mustang. At the Winternationals, he won his class after his opponent was disqualified.

Bill Ireland set the C/SA record in April 1965 with an ET of 13.68. This may be the first Mustang to appear in the record books. Bill won the Division 6 Stock crown in 1965. In 1966, he won the Street title in another Mustang, while his wife, Diane, drove this one to the Stock division title. (Photo Courtesy Michael Pottie)

This Michigan-based Mustang Stocker debuted in mid-1965 and was campaigned by a group of Ford engineers. Stark Hickey had three dealerships in Michigan. The west dealership was located on 7 Mile in Detroit. (Photo Courtesy Don Plungis)

The Drag Council

Having been formed in 1962 as part of the Performance and Economy Division, the Drag Council predates the Mustang by a few years. Dave Evans initially managed the division before being replaced by Charles Gray. Jacques Passino was the big boss over them all.

With the departure of Robert McNamara from Ford, people with a clearer vision began to recognize the growing youth market and decided to start manufacturing a more exciting line of cars. As early as 1960, Dave Evans had overseen the development of the 360-hp 352 engine, Ford's first high-performance engine since 1957. Evans had authorized the Experimental Vehicles Garage to prepare at least one car for under-the-radar forays into organized competition on drag strips.

After Dick Brannan soundly defeated all comers, including two factory-prepared Fords at a big Super/Stock race at Detroit Dragway with his dealer-prepared 1962 Galaxie, he was hired by Ford as the drag racing coordinator. Dick helped Ford select members for the Drag Council. The original members were Brannan, Phil Bonner, Gas Ronda, Les Ritchey, Len Richter, Ed Martin, Bob Tasca Sr., Jim Price, and Jerry Alderman.

The Drag Council remained at 10 or 11 members in 1963 and 1964. Mickey Thompson came aboard in 1963 and stayed through 1964 when Ford coined the marketing phrase "Total Performance." The council members were the lucky guys who received their cars for $1 and were given factory support for their racing efforts.

In 1965, Al Joniec and Tom Grove were added to the A/FX Mustang team. Although other racers received factory deals, they were not considered Drag Council members. After 1966, the Drag Council terminology seems to have disappeared.

It was a very good year for the Mustang, on the street and the strip. The manufacturer had accomplished what it had set out to do: establish a new performance leader. In A/FX and the emerging world of heads-up match racing, the Mustang was proving to be the car to beat. Chrysler and its altered wheelbase was briefly thought of as the be-all and end-all, but it held nothing over the Mustang. Things only got better.

This was Ronda's first 1965 A/FX Mustang. It was totaled at Lions Drag Strip on May 23 after it snapped an axle at speed and rolled numerous times. Ronda was okay and back in action a few weeks later with a new Mustang. (Photo Courtesy Forrest Bond)

Trophy girl Carol Doda at Half Moon Bay on this day was a dancer at one of the North Beach topless bars. Gaspar looks a bit embarrassed as he poses with her to get his regional Eliminator win recognition. (Photo Courtesy Forrest Bond)

Joe Davis and Wes Ingram were a team that relied upon the clean lines of the Mustang to get the job done. The Colt 45 began life running B/Altered with a 1938 Fiat Topolino body before they made the switch in late 1964. I hate to say it, but this one ran a Chevy mill. (Photo Courtesy Forrest Bond)

This Monroeville, Pennsylvania–based 1965 Mustang tore up the track in C/Gas Supercharged. I'm unsure what's under the hood, but 11.60 ETs were competitive. Note the four-lug front wheels, denoting that it was an original 6-cylinder Mustang. (Photo Courtesy Forrest Bond)

The Cammer

Introduced in 1965, without a doubt, the SOHC 427 is the most exotic domestic engine ever produced. Why was the engine developed in the first place? Well, the stark reality is because on NASCAR's big oval tracks, the hi-rise 427 couldn't compete with the Chrysler Hemi. Not willing to settle for second, Ford set out to rectifying the situation. The Cammer went from the drawing board to completion in just 90 days. To keep costs to a minimum the engineering team, led by Norm Faustyn, built the Cammer upon the existing 427. To handle the increased power of the twin overhead cams, the bottom end was supported with cross-bolted mains, a crossed-drilled forged crank, forged pistons, rods, and an improved oiling system.

Take your pick: the Boss 429 (left), the 4.6L Cobra (middle), or the SOHC 427 (right). Whichever you chose, you come up a winner.

The cast-iron heads featured gargantuan 2.25-inch hollow-stem intake valves and 1.90-inch sodium-filled exhaust valves. To rotate the two cams, Ford went with a gear-driven chain that when laid out, measured 6 feet in length.

Cast-iron rockers mounted on a hardened steel shaft actuated the valves. Valve lash adjustment on the early Cammers was by lash adjusters, but a later design saw this changed to adjusting screws. The void cam space within the block was filled with a dummy shaft that operated the oil pump and dual-point distributor. A separate chain ran the shaft off the crank.

Covering the maze of gears and chain was a two-piece aluminum cover with removable access plates. The engine could out-rev a Hemi, peaking at around 10,000 rpm, while out the door, horsepower was pegged at 650. Production of the Cammer ended in 1967. Just think: if NASCAR President Bill Frances hadn't reneged on his approval of the SOHC 427, drag racers may never have enjoyed the benefits.

1966: Stepping Up the Game

With Mustang sales well beyond expectations, the manufacturer saw little reason to mess with the car in 1966. It was a wise decision, as it sold another 607,000 units. With Ford now fully committed to "Race on Sunday," it expanded its drag race efforts. Leading the charge was the Mustang, which proved to be a force in every category from Stock to Factory Experimental.

The Shelby Mustang became the Shelby GT350 in 1966, and if the 306-hp 289 wasn't enough for you, there was always the Paxton supercharger option. Carroll Shelby and company built 11 such beasts, which produced a reported 395 hp. The option added a hefty $670 to the price of a GT350.

Hot rodders and drag racers alike found better ways of improving performance for the money. Of course, the ones we're most interested in here are the ones that showed up on the nation's drag strips. Shelby built four Mustangs in both 1965 and 1966 specifically for drag race purposes. These cars ran in the Sports Production category and set numerous class records.

Long-Nose Mustangs

Taking the two altered-wheelbase Mustangs of 1965 to the next level were the six long-nose Mustangs produced by Holman-Moody. Five of the cars went to the Drag Team members Dick Brannan, Gas Ronda, Bill Lawton, Phil Bonner, and Tommy Grove, while the sixth car appears to have stayed with Holman-Moody or Ford. These Mustangs were an integral part of the Funny Car evolution and could be looked at as the bridge between the earlier Factory Experimental cars and the full-blown, tube-chassis, flip-up Funny Cars that Mercury first introduced in 1966.

The first built was the Tasca *Mystery 9*, which was the prototype for the remainder of cars and constructed using a body in white. All of the Mustangs were built upon a 2x3 chrome-moly chassis with a wheelbase of 112 inches (4 inches over the production Mustang). This wheelbase

Below: *This group photo was taken prior to the 1966 NHRA Winternationals. Pictured (front to back) are Bill Ireland, Ed Terry, Gas Ronda, Mike Schmitt, and Les Ritchey. The lone dragster belongs to Connie Kalitta.*

You didn't need to be Superman to hoist this fiber-glass shell of the Holman-Moody Mustang. The completed long-nose cars were said to weigh under 2,200 pounds.

Here, late in 1965, Ronda's long-nose Mustang takes shape at Holman-Moody's. In true Funny Car fashion, there were 15 inches of front-end length added between the engine and the front spindle.

*Tasca's **Mystery 9** was said to have been the first long-nose Mustang built. Helping to gain traction here at Cecil County were Goodyear slicks and an ample amount of rosin. Filling the 9-inch rear were 4:10 or 4:30 gears. For stopping power, the Mustang relied upon rear brakes only and a Diest chute. (Photo Courtesy Michael Pottie)*

Repeat Wins

The year 1966 proved to be pretty much a repeat of 1965 with Mustangs winning all the major events. In January, Charlie Gray tried to have the Mustangs homologated to run NHRA A/FX with no luck. Instead, the NHRA placed the cars in C/Fuel Dragster, where at the Winternationals, Ronda and his Mustang took class with a 9.51.

Meanwhile, in the Street Eliminator final, Jerry Harvey took Len Ritcher's old Cammer Mustang to the category final, where he defeated the B/FX Galaxie of Mike Schmitt. At the AHRA Winternationals, Brannan set low ET and top speed with a 9.21 at 149.50 mph and won the Unlimited Stock category, while Lawton took the Mr. Stock Eliminator title. At the same race, Les Ritchey won Super Stock in his A/FX-legal Mustang, running a 10.44 in defeating the Mustang of Tommy Grove. Wrapping up the winter meets was the NASCAR show in Florida, where Bill Lawton, driving the Tasca *Mystery 9*, won the Grand National Stock title.

On went the season. Gas Ronda was back in the headlines in March after winning the Funny Car Eliminator at the U.S. Fuel and Gas Championship at Bakersfield. Ronda's Mustang became the first unblown Funny Car to turn an 8-second time when he defeated the Barracuda

was set by extending the front end (hence, the long-nose moniker) forward 15 inches.

Each car was fitted with the twisted leaf front suspension, although Tasca later switched to a tube axle. The rear suspension was slid 10 inches forward. The 9-inch rear was supported by adjustable traction arms and leaf springs. To help the 11-inch slicks grip the track, the Cammer was moved rearward 15 inches. Weighing 2,200 pounds, the new cars were approximately 1,000 pounds lighter than a 1965 A/FX Mustang.

As seen here in the Jerry Harvey Mustang, the engine bay was wall-to-wall Cammer. Ram tubes drew cool air from the grille, while the bubbled hood expelled the hot underhood air. The cowl-mounted gauge monitored fuel pressure. (Photo Courtesy Michael Pottie)

of Sox & Martin in the class final with an 8.96 at 155.97 mph. Tommy Grove won NHRA's first Funny Car Eliminator (S/XS) at the Springnationals running 8.70s (and handing Ronnie Sox another final round loss) before going on to win Comp Eliminator.

By late summer, Ronda's Mustang was cranking out times of 174 mph. To produce these numbers, Gas relied upon Les Ritchey's Performance Associates to prepare the SOHC 427, which pumped out in the neighborhood of 660 hp. Internal goodies for the SOHC engine included 0.586-inch-lift Crane Cams, Mickey Thompson rods, and 12:1 compression. Topping the mill were 13-inch Hilborn injector stacks feeding a dose of nitro. A Scintilla magneto with 32- to 38-degrees of advance lit the Ford's fire. The 4-speed transmission proved to be a handful in these ever-quickening Funny Cars, and by midseason, everyone was making the switch to automatics. Ronda went with the new-for-1966 C-6 transmission and closed the season by winning the AHRA Championship.

Harvey won Street Eliminator at the 1966 NHRA Winternationals by defeating the Galaxie of Mike Schmitt in the final with an ET of 10.68 at 132.15 mph. (Photo Courtesy Michael Pottie)

Ford's Cammer was an all-out race engine that was never available in a street-driven car. The engine was available to the general public who could purchase one through Ford between the years 1965 and 1967. The price was approximately $2,500. Injectors were becoming standard equipment on the match race cars, as seen here on Gas Ronda's long-nose Mustang.

There was no longer a comparison between the Mustang interior and that on the match race exhibition cars. The sturdy Holman-Moody roll cage was required safety gear.

This is a look at the twisted leaf suspension under the long-nose Mustang. This one belongs to Gas Ronda's Mustang. The car was restored by Eric Lindberg and the crew at Hite Autobody in 2006. (Photo Courtesy Zach Straits)

Gas Ronda's ties to Ford put him behind the wheel of the long-nose Mustang in 1966. At the Smokers meet in Bakersfield, the Mustang became the first unblown Funny Car to turn an 8-second ET, when Gas put away the Barracuda of Sox & Martin with an 8.96 at 155.97 mph.

Tommy Grove campaigned his long-nose Mustang into 1967. He surprised many when he continuously defeated the new flip-top Funny Cars with the aging Mustang. (Photo Courtesy Michael Pottie)

By the time Phil Bonner retired his stretched Mustang late in 1967, the car was capable of 8.70 ETs. Phil won the 2,400-pound Funny Car class at the AHRA Nationals in 1967. (Photo Courtesy Michael Pottie)

Ronda showed many Hemi Mopars the way home. Here, he defeats the Southern California Plymouth Dealers-sponsored rear-engine Hemi 'Cuda driven by Tom McEwen. These cars ran in the 170-mph range. (Photo Courtesy Michael Pottie)

Experimental Stock

In the next phase of the Funny Car evolution was the Experimental Stock (XS) cars of 1966. Branching off from Factory Experimental, the category initially consisted of five classes: A through E. The A Supercharged (S/XS) class was later added specifically for blown cars.

Nitromethane was permitted in S/XS and A/XS only, as were tube chassis (100-inch minimum). There was no cubic-inch limit in the two upper classes, but the lower-class cars were limited to 430 ci and carburation. These B through E classes competed in NHRA's Street Eliminator, while the S and A/XS competed in Comp Eliminator. Class breakdowns were based upon weight and were as follows: S/XS and A/XS, 2,000 pounds; B/XS, 2,600 pounds; C/XS, 3,000 pounds; D/XS, 3,200 pounds; and E/XS, 3,400 pounds.

Mike Burns, racing director at Mel Burns Ford, prepped and ran this AHRA record-holding Shelby Mustang. The photo was snapped outside the dealership. Mel Burns was an authorized Shelby dealer located in Long Beach, California. Shelby produced 2,380 Mustangs in 1966; of those, 936 were purchased by the Hertz car rental company. A number of these cars were rented to weekend racers and a few less-scrupulous souls are known to have swapped the 289 with a bread-and-butter 289 during the rental period. (Photo Courtesy Michael Pottie)

Hue Baby Climbs Aboard

The Georgia Shaker, Hubert Platt, was enjoying success racing his home-built stretched-out Mustang that he debuted in the fall of 1965. Hubert built the match racer at home with the help of fellow racer Paul Yates in a matter of 10 days. His Mustang had the rear suspension bumped up 2 inches, and the 2x3 chassis extended the front 14 inches. A 427 Wedge saw the Mustang eventually

Hubert Platt couldn't get his hands on a factory long-nose Mustang, so he built his own. The Wedge-powered car saw low-9-second times before it was wrecked. It was replaced with a 143-inch-wheelbase fiberglass Mustang. (Photo Courtesy Steve Reyes)

When Dick Brannan took a hiatus from driving after wrecking his Ultra Stock Mustang, he turned the reins of his long-nose Mustang to Hubert Platt. Platt raced the car into 1967, recording best ETs in the 8.30s. (Photo Courtesy Allen Platt)

record low-9-second times.

To compete with the new flip-up funnies appearing on the scene, Platt had Pat Foster at Race Car Specialties build him a one-piece fiberglass Mustang early in 1966. Unlike the Holman-Moody long-nose Mustangs, this one featured a straight-axle front end and a 143-inch wheelbase. Although the one-piece body, which was formed by mating Cal Automotive panels, didn't flip-up like the Comets, it could easily be removed by two people. An injected and stroked Cammer supplied the estimated 650 hp to an Art Carr–prepared C-6 transmission and 4:11 rear gears. Foster and Platt did their homework and managed to get the car's weight to less than 1,800 pounds.

Hubert ran the Mustang for a little more than two months in mid-1966 before taking over the controls of Dick Brannan's long-nose Mustang. Brannan had crashed the Mustang in April, and with pressure from Ford, the Drag Team boss resigned himself to the sidelines. Platt proceeded to win the AHRA Nationals in 1966 before selling the car to Larry Coleman in January 1967.

Hubert continued to drive the Mustang through the middle of the year, winning A/XS at the 1967 NHRA Winternationals and the NASCAR Summernationals. In May, Brannan called on Platt once again, this time bringing him to Detroit to test out the 1967 427-powered Fairlane. Platt took his last ride in the Mustang in May during a failed match race against his brother Huston in the *Dixie Twister* Camaro. A blown head gasket sidelined Hubert after the first round.

Time to Refocus

Although the so-called heads-up Mustang (a Funny Car for all intents and purposes) was the center of Ford's focus through much of 1966, the manufacturer was beginning to redirect its attention elsewhere. The Funny Car category was becoming a dangerous place, as exploding parts and injuries were happening all too frequently. By mid-1966, Ford was looking to refocus its drag racing efforts away from the Funny Car and back to production-based cars.

In 1966, Ford produced 57 NHRA-legal R-Code XL-500 Fairlanes. The medium-riser engine produced a

Larry Coleman was just one of many names to flank this Holman-Moody A/FX Mustang. First up was Dick Brannan, followed by Hubert Platt, Coleman, and then Chester Andrews. Larry added a blower to the Cammer in 1967 and put Sid Foster in the seat. When Larry moved into a flip-up Torino, he took the blown Cammer from the Mustang with him. (Photo Courtesy Lou Hart)

rated 425 hp and proved to be an immediate success on both the street and the strip. The 427 Fairlane returned in 1967 as Ford's top performer and was now available in both twin 4-barrel and single 4-barrel (410-hp) configurations. Total production through 1967 was 229 units, with another 60 Mercury Comets being produced.

By mid-1966, the Mustang was the dominant car in heads-up Funny Car. However, the manufacturer was looking to sell cars, so it refocused its attention on cars that the public could actually buy. Gaining ground was easy when you had guys such as Walt Wilson, whose 1966 Mustang was the scourge of AHRA Middle Stock. Walt campaigned the Mustang into 1967 and collected something like 98 class trophies. Times in the 12.70s were common. (Photo Courtesy Walt Wilson)

Ford's top Stock and Super Stock performer in 1966 and 1967 was the 427-powered Fairlane. Tom Schumacher's 1966 model was number-5 of 50 produced with the twin-Holley 425-hp 427.

CHAPTER 2

1967-1968
COMPETITION
BREEDS SUCCESS

With Ford sticking to its practice of giving its model lines a facelift every two years, the Mustang received a slight revamping in 1967. Sales remained high in the face of competition from the newly released pony cars: the Chevy Camaro, Pontiac Firebird, and Mercury Cougar. Putting them to shame, Ford sold approximately 470,000 Mustangs in 1967, which was more than the Camaro, Firebird, and Cougar combined.

Detroit's bigger is better mentality saw Ford add inches to the Mustang's dimension and approximately 90 pounds to its weight. Added to the options list was the 390-ci engine, which produced 320 hp. Although it was a decent street brawler, the 390 Mustang failed to make an impression in class competition on the track due in large part to its weak valve springs, which limited RPM. By 1968, any performance concerns that buyers may have had were erased with the release of the Cobra Jet Mustang.

1967: Pony Express

Factory support began to wane in the Experimental Stock category as Ford turned its attention toward the new NHRA Super Stock category. Although, the so-called

TOP LEFT: *Ford and Mercury merged their racing programs in 1967, and most of the factory drivers were in Cobra Jet Mustangs at the 1968 Winternationals. Don Nicholson ran SS/EA with this one but fell in the second round when the 428 engine spun a bearing. The Mustang was a one-race-only car for Don and was sold to Tom Safford prior to the Winternationals.*

The Mustang lost some gloss to the 427 Fairlane in 1967, as its top-billing 390-ci engine came up short in the performance department. This 1967 390-ci GT is running D/S here at Dover Dragstrip in 1968.

Bill Ireland began the year in a CJ-powered Torino before making the switch to a CJ-powered Mustang. The Mustang began life with a 390-ci engine but, being a member of Ford's Drag Council, a swap to 428 was made at the factory. Holman-Moody was called to make the necessary modifications just as it had on the original six factory drag Mustangs. (Photo Courtesy Larry Pfister)

Funny Cars in S/XS held the most fan appeal and pulled in the most wins for the Mustang. Beyond their outside appearance, Funny Cars shared very little with the showroom models that Ford was trying to sell.

The Birth of Super Stock

The new Super Stock category consisted of 10 classes for cars no older than 1962. Class designations were SS/A through SS/E, and SS/AA through SS/EA for automatic transmission–equipped cars. Unlike Stock, Super Stock rules were fairly liberal and permitted the use of any stock configuration intake manifold, any camshaft, and any slick that fit the stock wheel well. The rules also stated that cars ran off established class records, and if you ran quicker than 0.10 under the record during eliminations,

BOTTOM LEFT: *The* **Phony Pony** *of Junior Brogdon was built around an early drag chassis. The narrow fiberglass Mustang at one time ran twin injected 289 engines. Its best times were in the 8.30s. (Photo Courtesy Steve Reyes)*

you automatically lost. That is, unless the other driver ran farther under the established class record. Although the 1967 Mustang wasn't the best fit, Ford did lead with its twin 4-barrel-equipped 427 Fairlane in SS/B and the single 4-barrel version of the same engine in SS/C. Contracted drivers Hubert Platt, Ed Terry, Bill Ireland, among others, found themselves in a Super Stock Fairlane in 1967.

The Drag Team Divides

The look of Experimental Stock (Funny Car) changed dramatically in 1967 as both Ford and Chrysler moved many of its contracted drivers to Super Stock. The reason was twofold: (1) the learning curve and search for more power in Funny Cars saw the frequency of exploding blowers and transmissions becoming too common, and (2) too many drivers were getting hurt. The second reason was easy to see. In addition, the Super Stocks actually looked like the cars the manufacturers were trying to sell.

Gas Ronda, Tommy Grove, and the crew at Tasca Ford maintained their standing in Funny Car when they each debuted new Cammer-powered fiberglass Mustangs early in the season. While flip-up bodies were now seemingly the way to go, Ronda, who was AHRA's Funny Car driver of the year in 1967, went with a two-piece body riding on a 118-inch wheelbase Exhibition Engineering chassis. Grove and Tasca each chose flip-up Mustangs mounted to Logghe chassis.

Gas Ronda debuted a new Mustang late in the summer of 1967. The Cammer initially ran injected before Gas made the switch to a blower late in the season and knocked out 7.60 times. With the death of close friend and engine builder Les Ritchey, Gas turned to Ed Pink to build his engines. Gas found that the blown motor overpowered the Exhibition Engineering chassis. He debuted a new Mustang in 1969. (Photo Courtesy Eric English)

Don't Forget the Long-Nose

The long-nose Mustang of 1966 wasn't dead yet, as Hubert Platt gave his aging Brannan Mustang a major victory when he won A/XS (the 2,000-pound class) at the NHRA Winternationals. In B/XS, a 2,400-pound class, Bill Lawton brought home the gold in Tasca's long-nose Mustang. Tommy Grove, in one of the last outings of his long-nose Ford Charger surprised many when he won the NHRA Springnationals, which was a race attended by the favored flip-up Mercury Comets of Ed Schartman and Don Nicholson.

Ed Pink laid his hands on Gas Ronda's Cammer and made it a winner. Hilborn was the go-to for injectors. The fuel feed was split between the injectors and direct to the ports. (Photo Courtesy Eric English)

In the Funny Car final, Tommy defeated the blown Cammer-powered Cougar of Maynard Rupp and Roy Steffey. At the preceding Super Stock Nationals, Grove was the big winner on all three days of the event, taking

Tasca's Mystery 9 became the Mystery 8 in the summer of 1966 when Bill Lawton ran 8.60 times while defeating the Hemi Dart of Charlie Allen in a best-of-three match race. A larger fuel pump and injectors modified by mechanic John Healey received credit for the magical times. (Photo Courtesy Michael Pottie)

The final year for the lower Experimental Stock classes (B through E) was 1967. Jerry Harvey's previous Winternationals-winning SOHC Mustang has been relegated to C/XS here at the 1967 Winternationals. (Photo Courtesy Michael Pottie)

For each big-name Funny Car being campaigned, there was a multitude of not-so-familiar Funny Cars competing coast to coast, one being Bob Blinn's 1967 Contemporary Fiberglass-sponsored Mustang. Blinn's Mustang driven by Bud Fazone recorded ETs of 8.50 at close to 170 mph, before he made the switch from injection to a blower. The Azusa, California–based Mustang featured an SOHC engine and an Art Carr TorqueFlite transmission in a Sammy Vildo chassis. (Tom West Photography/Lou Hart Archives)

The bearing issue wasn't unique to Al, as several Cammers were having the same issue. The problem was solved by widening the journals and running 392 Chrysler Hemi bearings. After a crash at the Super Stock Nationals in 1966, the *Batcar* went back to Holman-Moody, where it received the altered wheelbase, long-nose treatment. At the end of the 1967 season, Al reinvented the *Batcar* as the *Hairy One* and campaigned it through 1968 with its blue electrostatic-applied furry finish.

After the Super Stock Nationals, the Tasca team won Julio Marra's King of Kings race at Capitol Raceway. The injected Mustang recorded 8.20 times to defeat a field that consisted of all blown cars. Shortly after the King of Kings, Tasca replaced the injected engine with a new blown motor. Tasca's crew chief/engine builder John Healey admitted having issues keeping the Cammer alive with a blower. He found that the solution was to get more fuel into the mill.

Revolutionizing the Gas Category

The Gas category, which was dominated for the first half of the decade by Willys and Anglias, took on a new look in 1967 as "Ohio" George Montgomery and his Cammer-powered Mustang, revolutionized the category.

George signed with Ford late in 1965 after he and his Chevy-powered 1933 Willys lost AA/GS at the NHRA Nationals. Ford's Charlie Gray had been bugging him to sign for some time, initially offering him a 289. George had no interest in the small motor and held out for an SOHC 427.

With the Cammer being in short supply, Ford did its best and sent him the engine in pieces as they became available. Backing the Cammer in the Willys was a Ford-prepped C-6 transmission that shifted automatically at 8,800 rpm, allowing George to literally stab and steer. The Willys was the first drag car to be placed in Ford's wind tunnel. The car created 600 pounds of lift in the rear, causing it to nearly slide off its pedestal.

the 2,400-pound Funny Car class while recording 8.30 times. Other Mustangs in the winner's circle that weekend were the Tasca Ford and Al Joniec.

Al's *Batcar* began as a class-legal A/FX car powered by a 427 Wedge. He received the SOHC 427 shortly after its debut, and by the time the Nationals rolled around, the car was turning 10.60s. Al was chewing up main bearings left and right on Indy weekend and fell out of contention.

All of George Montgomery's drag cars could have easily doubled as show cars. The quality and finish was that good. (Photo Courtesy John Vanderpryt)

George debuted the Cammer Willys in May, and from the get-go it was a winner. It won its class at the NHRA Springnationals in June and on Labor Day at the Nationals, where it ran a 9.34.

In 1966, when one of Ford's vice presidents viewed the Cammer-powered Willys, he said, "Nice, but we sell Fords, don't we?"

That all but spelled the end of the Willys. A fiberglass Cal-Automotive Mustang shell was procured, and as Gasser rules at the time dictated that the car had to run an OEM chassis, the Mustang body was mounted on George's existing 1933 Willys chassis.

At its Springnationals debut, the Mustang dropped more than a few jaws. Tech inspectors took one look at the car and said, "No way!"

The head of NHRA tech, Farmer Dismuke, who had been kept abreast of the build all along stepped in and gave the car the A-Okay. The Malco Gasser went on to win AA/G with an astounding 8.94 at 160.56 mph. The 'Stang owned the class, setting the record in June with an 8.93 at 162.16 mph and resetting it a few times before George retired the car at the end of 1968.

1968: Attack of the Cobra Jet

Another year of cosmetic change saw the Mustang take on a cleaner look with a slight revamp of the grille and side scoop layout. In an exploding pony car market, Ford still managed to sell more than 300,000 Mustangs.

George Montgomery's Cammer-powered Mustang recorded an AA/G record-setting ET of 8.93 at 162.16 mph. Note that the gas lines fed to both the Hilborn injectors and to the manifold. The magnesium 6-71 blower housing was manufactured for George. (Photo Courtesy John Vanderpryt)

"Ohio" George Montgomery's evolutionary Mustang rode on a modified Willys chassis with a 110-inch wheelbase. George stated that the Mustang rode like a Rolls-Royce compared to his old 1933 Willys. (Photo Courtesy Michael Mihalko)

Ed Terry ran an SS/C Fairlane at the 1967 Winternationals where, to the joy of many, he defeated the Camaro of Grumpy Jenkins in the first round of eliminations. Ed received his Cobra Jet Mustang after the 1968 Winternationals. In March, he won his class at the Hot Rod magazine meet. (Photo Courtesy Charles Morris)

Running out of Hayward Ford in 1968, this sharp-looking 1966 Shelby Mustang was showing the competition it still had what it took to get the job done. Hayward was one of the nation's leading Shelby dealers. The bumper sticker states, "This is Ford Country . . . What Are You Driving?" (Photo Courtesy James Handy)

Ford laid to rest the Mustang's base 289 in December 1967 and replaced it with the new 302. Although no performance version of the engine was offered from the factory, Carroll Shelby added some performance goodies to the mill when he offered it in his GT350.

The big news for the Mustang came when the 428 Cobra Jet appeared on the options list. I think it's fair to say that Ford had finally turned the Mustang into a genuine performance leader. Would it be an overstatement to say that the world of drag racing would never be the same?

Ford Bares Its Fangs

Ford hit a home run when it unleashed the 428 Cobra Jet Mustang. And to think, if it hadn't been for the efforts of Rhode Island's Bob Tasca Sr. and a push from *Hot Rod* magazine, the car probably never would have been produced.

For a manufacturer that touted "Total Performance," Ford's share of the performance market had dwindled to less than 8 percent by the end of 1967. Tasca could see the need for a car that would put Ford back in the run. Enter the Tasca-built KR-8 (King of the Road) 428 Mustang. The KR-8 was built using Bob's personal 390-equipped 1967 Mustang coupe.

When the 390 suddenly expired, Bob chose the opportunity to drop in a Police Interceptor 428. Before taking its place in the Mustang, the engine was stuffed with proven performance 406–427 parts pulled from Ford's well-stocked parts bin. In November of 1967, *Hot Rod* magazine ran a feature article on Tasca's Mus-

tang and encouraged its readers to send the magazine-provided ballot to Henry Ford II demanding the solid 13-second car be built.

Ford heard the cries and built a total of 1,299 CJ-powered Mustangs through the remainder of the 1968 model year. In addition, the engine found its way into 517 Shelby GT500 KR Mustangs, 22 Fairlanes, 37 Mercury Cougars, and several Comets. Ford gave the engine a low-ball rating of 335 hp, which the NHRA saw through and added another 10 hp at the end of the season.

Holman-Moody-Stroppe

Six Wimbledon White Cobra Jet Mustangs were shipped to Holman-Moody-Stroppe to be specially prepared for their Winternationals debut on February 2. Classes run were C/S and C/SA, two cars in SS/E, and two in SS/EA. Eventually, a total of 50 Cobra Jet Mustangs (numerically sequenced above the 6 WN cars) were prepped for drag race competition. Modifications to the Stock class cars included the use of forged 427 connecting rods, forged pistons squeezing out 11:0.1 compression, a C8AX-C camshaft (0.500 lift, 282 duration), a dual-point distributor, Jardine headers, a battery that was relocated to the trunk, 4.44 gears, traction bars, Goodyear slicks,

While Ford wanted him to continue racing Super Stock with his Winternationals Mustang, Phil Bonner had other ideas. He replaced the 428 with an SOHC 427 and match raced the wheels off the car. Factory support for Phil ended after the 1968 season. (Photo Courtesy Eric English)

Like many of the factory lightweight Mustangs built, Al's Super Stock winner has been restored. The 735-cfm Holley carburetor draws air from a functioning Ram Air scoop.

By winning Super Stock at the NHRA Winternationals, Al Joniec gave Ford its first-ever NHRA Super Stock title. A 427 later replaced the 428, and Al did a fair amount of match racing with the car. (Photo Courtesy Charles Morris)

and staggered shocks for the 4-speed cars. The Super Stock cars included all of the Stock modifications plus a high-flow aluminum intake manifold, C8AX-D camshaft (0.600 lift, 330 duration), Crane springs, a three-point roll bar, and Goodyear slicks mounted on Cragar S/S rims.

Five team drivers drove the six cars: Gas Ronda, Don Nicholson, Jerry Harvey, Al Joniec, and Hubert Platt. Platt drove a C/SA car and an SS/E car and made it to the class final in each.

As expected, the Mustangs dominated with the SS/E class final coming down to the Mustangs of Platt and Al Joniec. Platt red-lighted and ran an 11.58 while Al took the win with a 12.12 at 109.48 mph. The pair met up again in Super Stock Eliminator, as Platt's previous low ET found him back in the running, but this time the fix was in.

Hubert Platt lays out the Hemi GTX of Sox & Martin on the way to a class final at the Winternationals in 1968. Platt also wheeled a C/SA Cobra Jet Mustang at the meet. (Photo Courtesy Steve Reyes)

This underside shot of Hubert Platt's 1968 Mustang shows the trimming that was done to the leaf springs to move them inboard to gain additional room for the Goodyear slicks. (Photo Courtesy Rusty Gillis)

Hubert Platt's SS/E Cobra Jet Mustang that played runner-up at the Winternationals received an eye-popping metal-flake silver and black paint job in the spring. The car was later heavily damaged when it crashed and rolled at Dallas. It was repaired and passed on to Randy Payne.

This photo just doesn't do the new, heavy metal-flake paint on Hubert Platt's Mustang justice. Thompson Body Shop in Alpharetta, Georgia, must be given credit. Sadly, the paint didn't last. (Photo Courtesy Marvin T. Smith)

Before the race, the decision was made by the Ford representatives on hand that the winner would be decided on a coin toss. Hubert lost the toss, giving the win to Joniec. Just a little peeved, Platt took the red light and crossed the finish line first.

Al waded through eliminations and faced the SS/DA Mopar of Dave Wren in the final. It proved to be an anticlimactic ending, as Dave, running the quicker car, had to spot Al a slight lead. Feeling the pressure and knowing he was going to have a tough time playing catch-up,

Dave cut the light a little too quick and fouled away any chance of winning. The race was over on the starting line, and Al earned Ford its first-ever Super Stock title.

With records and class wins under its belt, the production Cobra Jet Mustang arrived in showrooms on April 1 as a proven winner. Beyond the four class wins at the Winternationals, the Cobra Jet Mustang dominated through the remainder of the season.

Here's just a sample of its first-year accomplishments: Hubert Platt set the SS/E class record at Phenix City in

Here is the result of a bad run at Southeastern International Dragway in Dallas, Georgia. Hubert walked away. The Mustang was repaired, painted white, and briefly campaigned by Randy Payne before being sold to Rusty Gillis. (Photo Courtesy Marvin T. Smith)

The Tasca Cobra Jet Mustang began as a 4-speed car, but one too many broken transmissions forced the team switch to a C-6. Bill Lawton was a great driver and drove the team's Funny Car simultaneously with the Super Stock car.

Tom Safford, driving Dyno Don's old Mustang, was a heavy hitter from the West Coast, winning several big races at Lions and Orange County International Raceway (OCIR) during the late 1960s and early 1970s. (Photo Courtesy Lou Hart)

Jerry Harvey, SS/E class winner at Indy in 1968, ran with the so-called Canadian heads. Jerry drove for Bob Ford until 1966, when his father, Paul Harvey, opened his own dealership. (Photo Courtesy Rob Potter)

April with an 11.67 ET at 120.96 mph. Jerry Harvey won SS/E in June at the Springnationals while Carl Holbrook's 12.59 won SS/FA. Barrie Poole set the ET record in SS/EA with an 11.87 at Indy in July. At the Nationals, Tony Rainero ran a 11.38 in SS/E to defeat Al Joniec during class runoffs.

At the time, Al's Cobra Jet was considered the quickest car in the nation. Three cars remained in class: Tony's car (driven by partner Frank Lundgren), Dave Lyall's car, and Jerry Harvey's car. As Tony relayed in a 428cobrajet. org article, unknown to him, Ford representatives took Frank aside for a talk. The NHRA had already stated that the final runs in eliminations would set the new index for the class. Ford, besides running for the manufacturers cup with the factory-supported cars, did not want the index lowered. Tony was unhappy with how Ford was trying to manipulate the outcome of the race after having been promised support previously but receiving none. After voicing his opinion to the representative on the lack of support for independents to the point of withholding parts, Tony was promised that if they agreed to throw the race, that would no longer be an issue.

With three Cobra Jet cars remaining, it was up to the racers how they wished to proceed. All that Ford wanted was one of its team cars in the winner's circle. Tony recalled that they ended up flipping a coin to determine the running order. Jerry won with the Paul Harvey car, and Dave was runner-up. Frank was out on Dave but followed through on the plan and fake a missed shift. As it turned out, at tear down, the Dave Lyall car was disqualified for having under-CC heads. Records show Paul Harvey as the class winner with a 12.12.

Additional wins and records followed through the remainder of the season. Further Nationals action saw H. J. Van Schoick win C/SA with his Cobra Jet. Ken McLellan reset the SS/E record in September at Amarillo with a 125.80 mph. Tom Safford and Roger Caster shared the SS/EA record beginning in September with an 11.86 and a 121.40 mph.

Experimental Stock Goes Full Funny

Although it was technically still referred to as Supercharged Experimental Stock, for all intents and purposes these cars were Funny Cars as we know them today. By this point in Funny Car evolution, all of the competitive

Chicago-based Bob DuBrock did pretty well running the AHRA and NASCAR Ultra Stock classes with his Mustang. The former **Mr. Ford's Aggravation** was powered by a 427 Wedge that grabbed a few class records. Bob later added injectors and a load of nitro to the mix. Eighteen inches were added to the chassis ahead of the firewall. (Photo Courtesy John Foster Jr.)

In 1967, Dick Loehr had a new Stampede Mustang Funny Car built. The car was unique in the sense that it was much lower than his competitors. The Mustang initially ran a Cammer before Dick made the switch to a 392 Chrysler Hemi. Loehr ran a best ET of 7.86 at 189.70 mph with the car at OCIR. Both Dick and his long-time crew chief John Skiba worked for Max Curtis Ford. (Photo Tom West Photography/Lou Hart Archives)

cars were running flip-up bodies and tube chassis. Class rules for 1968 stated that S/XS was for cars with blowers or excessive engine relocation and allowed for a minimum weight of 2,000 pounds. The NHRA carried over A/XS from 1967 but dropped the remaining Experimental Stock classes.

The Funny Car became a little funnier this year when Chrysler's Hemi started showing up with more frequency in non-Chrysler cars. Although the Cammer could out-breathe and out-rev the Hemi, weaknesses began to appear in the form of cracked blocks under increasing nitro loads. It was no doubt that the move away from the

The Mustang remained a popular choice in Funny Car, although more of them were powered by the Chrysler Hemi. John Eads's Boss Hoss II saw its success come by way of a Chrysler powerplant. (Photo Courtesy James Handy)

The Larry Barker-driven Ralph Snodgrass and Pat Mahnken AA/FA Mustang won Competition Eliminator at the 1967 Hot Rod magazine meet. The Psycho was originally campaigned as a Cammer-powered Fiat before being rebodied as a Mustang and fitted with a 427 Wedge engine. The car's best ETs were in the 8.50s. (Photo Courtesy Pat Mahnken Family Archives)

After Doug Cook crashed the Stone, Woods & Cook Dark Horse Mustang Funny Car at Alton Dragway in 1967, the team rebounded in 1968 with this car: the Ghost of Dark Horse 2. A Logghe chassis and Chrysler Hemi rode under the flip-up body. (Photo Courtesy Tom West Photography/Lou Hart Archives)

Cammer was helped by the fact that Ford ended production of the engine in 1967.

Longtime Ford racer Dick Loehr debuted his new *Stampede* Mustang Funny Car in 1967 with an SOHC 427, but by 1968, he had replaced the engine with an early Chrysler Hemi. He used the hybrid combination to win a countless number of match races throughout the year and the season-ending AHRA World Finals.

Stone, Woods & Cook, saw the *Dark Horse* Hemi Mustang Funny Car destroyed in a late-1967 wreck that nearly cost Doug Cook his life. The team returned in 1968 with the *Ghost of Dark Horse 2* and hired driver Lyle Fisher at the wheel. The car was competitive and quite successful running match races.

Counting on the Cammer

TASCA Ford, sticking with Cammer power, won Unlimited Fuel at NASCAR Winter Championship drags when Bill Lawton in the *Mystery 7* Mustang defeated the GTO of Arnie Beswick. Lawton, with John Healey pulling wrenches, had no problem setting low ET and top speed no matter where they ran, but he increasingly ran into breakage issues after swapping the Hilborns for a 6-71 huffer.

Gas Ronda swapped out the injectors on his Cammer early in the year for a 6-71 and dipped into the 7s for the first time. Ronda led the way in a battle between Top Fuel cars and Funnies at Irwindale, winning his three rounds with a best of 7.93 at 179.28 mph. With the passing of

Les Ritchey in May 1966, Gas was now counting on Ed Pink to build his Cammers and keep the wins coming.

Tommy Grove laid down Funny Car's quickest time to date when he recorded a 7.65 at 192.70 mph at Cecil County's Fuel Funny Car Showdown on May 18. The show consisted of eight of the top cars in the nation: the Chevys of "Jungle" Jim Liberman and Dick Bourgeois, the Pontiacs of Arnie Beswick and Roy Gay, the Comet of "Dyno" Don Nicholson, and the Mustang of Tasca Ford. While others had issues keeping their Cammers alive, Grove had no problem, claiming that his secret was lots of fuel and low compression.

In an interview by drag race historian Charles Morris, Tommy said, "When everyone else ran a pump that delivered 14 to 16 gallons per minute, I had one built that delivered 50 gallons per minute. Then, I dropped the compression down to 5:1 and slowed down the blower. I ran the supercharged engine six months without ever having a head off."

Tommy and the Mustang proved to be a picture of consistency, defeating the *Color Me Gone* Dodge of Roger Lindamood and Roy Gay's Firebird before facing Jungle Jim's Nova in the final. Liberman took a slight holeshot lead off the line, but his Chevy's 7.85 was no match for Grove's 7.65. A month later, Tommy improved on his record time with a 7.52 while defeating Liberman once again on the equivalent of a 65-percent-load of nitro.

Tasca debuted its flip-up Mustang Funny Car in the spring of 1967, where the injected Cammer produced 8.30 ETs. By the time the car was retired, it sported a 6-71 blower and was recording times in the 7.30s. The **Mystery 7's** *biggest win came at the 1967 Super Stock Nationals, where the team won the 2,000-pound Funny Car class. (Photo Courtesy Ed Aigner)*

When Gas Ronda moved into a long-nose Mustang, Bill Ireland purchased his A/FX Mustang. Bill initially campaigned the car in Factory Experimental, but by the time he was done with it in 1969, it was running A/MP. (Photo Courtesy Michael Pottie)

Tom Grove's 1967 Logghe-chassis Mustang recorded 8.30 ETs. It was unblown during its initial outing. However, it only got better. By the spring of 1968, Tom had the quickest Funny Car in the nation. (Photo Courtesy Steve Reyes)

Call it an omen, but not all Mustangs campaigned were Ford powered. Paula Murphy, drag racing's first female Funny Car pilot, put plenty of her male counterparts on the trailer with her Hemi Mustang. The Mustang was Paula's first venture into the world of Funny Cars in 1968, which was after she drove door cars for a number of years.

The Trojan Horse *Mustang of Fullerton and Solarie was one of the strongest injected SOHC-powered Funny Cars on the West Coast. The Logghe-built Mustang was driven by Larry Fullerton, who saw his star rise over the next decade. (Tom West Photography/Lou Hart Archives)*

Funny Car Popularity

The popularity of the Experimental Stock Funny Cars reached a fever pitch by the end of 1968. Who knew that within the next few years Funny Car would challenge Top Fuel as the sport's most popular category?

Through 1968, we had Funny Car circuits, and Funny Car–only programs. Some of the biggest included the Lions Drag Strip Unlimited Funny Car Spectacular, Capital Raceway's King of Kings, and the East and West Coast

A graduate from the Gasser classes, San Antonio, Texas-based Ray Doyon joined the Funny Car ranks around 1967, when he purchased the Fritz Callier/J. E. Kristek fastback Chevy II. Don Hardy built Ray's Old Glory Mustang, *which is seen here at Irwindale. Ray ran the Mustang as late as 1971 with a Chrysler Hemi. His forte was match racing, and he saw plenty of success in his travels. (Tom West Photography/Lou Hart Archives)*

Funny Car Championship races. It went on and on. Fans ate it up, and racers climbed on board. There was money to be made, and many Funny Cars were built to cash in

Dick "Poll Cat" Poll hailed from Southern California and began his Funny Car career with this ex-Gas Ronda fuel-injected Mustang. Dick added a blower to the SOHC 427, but due to the heavy weight of the body, it failed to produce the big numbers. Dick later took over Ronda's 1969 Mustang. (Tom West Photography/Lou Hart Archives)

The Souzas

The Souza Mustang ran a best of 8.70s with an injected Wedge and 7.90s with a blown Cammer. An Art Carr C-6 transmitted power to the coil-spring-supported rear. (Photo Courtesy James Handy)

The Souzas (Harold, Dave, and their dad) ran a low-dollar Experimental Stock Funny Car out of Hayward, California. The popular team built its Mustang to replace a Ford-powered 1933 Willys Gasser it had been campaigning.

From the fabricated chassis to body modifications to the built Algon-injected 427 Wedge, these guys did it all themselves—all in their well-equipped single-car garage. The Mustang more than held its own against the heavier Funny Cars and recorded consistent 8.70 times.

The Souzas swapped out the Wedge late in 1968 and installed a fuel-fed blown SOHC 427 that took the Mustang into the 7-second zone. Escalating costs saw the team retire from racing in 1970. Twenty-five years later, the nostalgia craze was in full bloom, and the brothers wanted in on the action. They headed out to where the Mustang was last known to rest, only to discover it had been scrapped just days before.

Truly a family effort, the Souzas were a talented bunch, and their Mustang was a much-feared car in Southern California. Algon injection sits atop the 427. A Vertex magneto supplied the spark. (Photo Courtesy James Handy)

on the popularity. Top Fuel pilot Art Malone, who won his share of national events, saw the writing on the wall and built himself a Mustang Funny Car. Funny Car was the fastest-growing category, and it was only going to get bigger and better.

It's A Gas, Supercharged

It was Ohio George and his Mustang that kicked open the door of Gas, signaling the end of the Willys' and Anglia's dominance. Hot on the heels of Ohio George came a slew of modern-day machinery. Mike Marinoff and Skip Hess were two who stepped up with Mustangs of their own and were dominant. Marinoff teamed with Jon Wamser and driver Bill Reeves to run AA/GS. At one point, they held the class record with an 8.90 ET at 166.66 mph.

Through to the mid-1960s, the team of Jim "Fireball" Shores and Skip Hess campaigned a supercharged 1949 Anglia Gasser that proved to be one of most successful cars in class. At the end of 1967, they chose to go their separate ways.

Skip stuck with Gas and, seeing the writing on the wall, built a gorgeous AA/GS 1968 Mustang. Ford supplied Skip with all he needed for the Mustang, including the SOHC 427. The car featured a Don Kirby chassis and a multi-hued orange paint by "Molly" Sanders that covered a fiberglass shell. Skip and the Mustang achieved a best ET of 8.32 at 168.75 mph. Although it was sponsored by Revell (the model car company), a kit of the car was never offered.

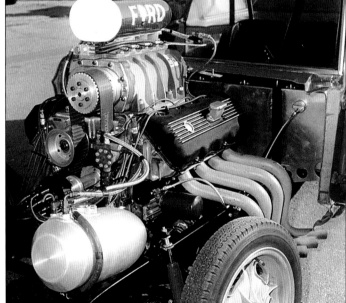

The AA/GS Mustang of Skip Hess debuted in 1968. Power came by way of an Ed Pink–built Cammer. Jim Kirby built the chassis, and the famed Rollin "Molly" Sanders applied the paint. The Mustang ran a best ET of 8.32 at 168.75 mph on gas and mid-7s at 180 mph on alcohol. Although it was sponsored by Revell, the company never made a kit of the car. (Photo Courtesy James Handy)

Nothing put the scare into the competition like a blown and injected SOHC 427. The tank up front held gas, feeding to the Hilborn four-port injection. (Photo Courtesy James Handy)

The heavily metal-flaked Mister Jim *was a popular B/Gas 1967 Mustang that was a regular at Dragway 42 in the latter half of the 1960s. Note the credit to David Meal on the lower rear quarter panel. David was involved with many of the successful Ohio Gassers in the 1960s. (Photo Courtesy Todd Wingerter)*

In October 1967, the Mike Marinoff and Jon Wamser AA/GS Mustang driven by Bill Reeves was the quickest car in class after recording an ET of 8.90 at 166.66 mph. Powering the car was an SOHC 427 stuffed with parts from Hilborn, Pete Robinson, ForgedTrue, Mickey Thompson, and Crane. (Photo Courtesy Dean Johnson)

Turbo-Stang

In 1962, Mechanical Engineer Gene Middlebrooks formed the company Turbonique and ran it out of his Florida home. What exactly was Turbonique? Well, it was an 850-hp micro-rocket engine that bolted to a car's differential. Several cars were built using the rocket turbine engine, including the *Black Widow* VW Bug that ran 183 mph before destroying itself, a 1965 Chevelle SS, an unreal go kart powered by twin Turbonique T-16 rockets, and the *Turbo-Stang*.

Giving the *Reader's Digest* condensed version, the micro-rocket/turbine ran off a monopropellant (rocket propulsion) fuel that carried the trade name of Thermolene. The fuel is sprayed into the combustion chamber at 600 psi and ignited by a single spark plug. As Thermolene will not ignite at low temps, oxygen is added through a separate inlet. When the fuse (plug) lit, acceleration comes instantly as the release of the hot gases spin the turbine. For a spectator, it had to have been quite the scene as the cars sat silent on the line, waiting for the tree to come down before lighting the plug. At the end of the run, power to the plug is shut off.

Like any good salesman, Gene Middlebrooks used the cars to help promote his mail-order Turbonique business. With advertisements in all the leading magazines, Joe Public filled out their order forms and mailed off their checks. The problem was that when "Joe" received his micro-rocket, it wasn't an easy bolt-in as Gene advertised. Customers were blowing themselves up trying to get the things to work. Fraud charges relating to Gene's refusal to reimburse dissatisfied customers finally brought down Turbonique. Two years in jail and a $4,000 fine followed.

Here at Great Lakes Dragway, Costilow faces the Turbine Dart of Gene Canham. Cal Custom formed the fiberglass Mustang body, while Lloyd Racing Enterprises in Harrisburg, Pennsylvania, was responsible for the build. (Photo Courtesy John Foster Jr.)

The rear end is flipped 180 degrees, and the turbine bolts directly to the pinion. The unit weighed 125 pounds. Horsepower was pegged at 850, which moved the Mustang to quarter-mile speeds approaching 160 mph. (Photo Courtesy John Foster Jr.)

Mr. Cal Automotive

At first glance, you'd never know what hid under the skin of Tex Collins's fiberglass Mustang. The Allisons reported 3,500 hpr was transmitted to the 1.90-ratio rear end through seven 12-inch clutch disks. Tex was also a Hollywood stunt man who worked on shows including **Rawhide** *and* **Gunsmoke** *and movies including* **A Fist Full of Dollars** *and* **It's a Mad, Mad, Mad, Mad World.** *(Tom West Photography/Lou Hart Archives)*

In 1965, Hollywood Badman Tex Collins purchased Cal Automotive (a fiberglass panel and body producer) from its founders, Bud Lang and Curt Hamilton. Tex owned a company called Ford Duplicators, which was contracted by Carroll Shelby to produce the fiberglass panels for his 1965 Mustangs. Early in 1965, Tex's elder son accidently burned the Ford Duplicator building down, which left Tex in a serious bind.

Needing a place to build the Shelby parts for Carroll, Tex bought the financially troubled Cal Automotive. To showcase the company, Tex built this unique Allison-powered fiberglass 1968 Mustang. The V-12 was salvaged from a P-51 Mustang and measured 1,710 ci. The flip-up fiberglass body with its removable front-end rode on a chrome-moly chassis that Tex designed and built himself. Tex modified the engine by installing a supercharger from an Allison-powered P-38 that provided 9½ pounds of boost.

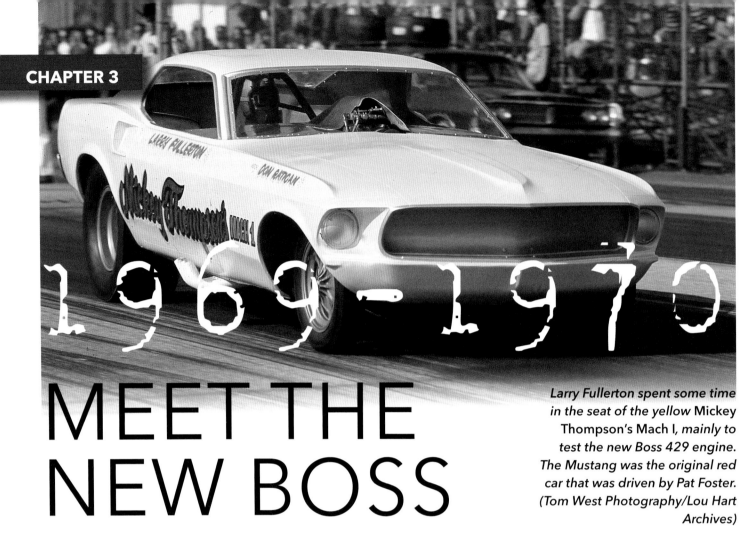

CHAPTER 3

1969-1970

MEET THE NEW BOSS

Larry Fullerton spent some time in the seat of the yellow Mickey Thompson's Mach I, *mainly to test the new Boss 429 engine. The Mustang was the original red car that was driven by Pat Foster. (Tom West Photography/Lou Hart Archives)*

With another cycle year upon the Mustang, the car received a make-over, and with it came an additional 4 inches in length and 150 pounds in weight. With its new quad headlights up front and a SportsRoof out back, the Mustang took on a tougher, more muscular appearance. A new performance model was added in the form of the Mach 1. Returning was the 428 Cobra Jet, which was joined this year by the Super Cobra Jet (SCJ) Drag Pak options that carried over into 1970.

The Drag Pak option got you a 3.90 or 4:30 rear gear, a beefy bottom end (rods, pistons, and crank), and an oil cooler to help keep temps down. These internal parts were specific to the SCJ and could not be interchanged (the SCJ was externally balanced) with the standard Cobra Jet. Horsepower ratings of the two engines were the same (335).

In 1969, Ford offered light valves and flat-top pistons for the 428 or dish pistons that came with heavy

The Cobra Jet Mustangs *dominated the mid–Super Stock categories north and south of the border. George Constantine and his Mach 1 out of Quebec, Canada, did his share of winning through 1972. (Photo Courtesy Rob Potter)*

valves. In 1970, the high compression and light valves weren't offered. Although the factory horsepower ratings remained unchanged, the NHRA made its adjustment.

1969: Upping the Ante

Joining the 428 in 1969 was a slew of new performance engines: the 351 Cleveland, the 302 H.O. (Boss 302), and the Blue Crescent (Boss) 429. Ram Air, which first appeared in 1968 on the Cobra Jet Mustang, was available in 1969 on the GT, Mach 1, and Shelbys, which were now being built inhouse. Buyers could apply the option to any engine from the 2-barrel 351 through the 428.

Of course, the NHRA refactored any combination using it, adding upward of 15 to 20 hp, which moved you up a class. Many racers instead stuck with a flat hood, as they found no real performance gain using the Ram Air. The performance version of the 351 Cleveland offered 10.7:1 compression and was rated at 290 hp. What made the Cleveland superior to any other engine in its class were the canted, oversize 2.19/1.71 valves.

The Big, Little Boss

The short-lived 302 H.O. was developed specifically for the Mustang (and found its way into 638 Cougars) to fit SCCA's Trans-Am rules that had a cubic inch limit of 305. The engine was only produced in 1969 and 1970 and featured the best parts Ford could fit into it. The high-nickel block was fitted with large-valve Cleveland heads, a 780 Holley carburetor, forged pistons, 10:5.1 compression, four-bolt mains, high-performance 289 connecting rods, and a solid cam featuring 0.477 lift. Rated at 290 hp, the Boss 302 accomplished what it set out to do, and that was to strip Chevy of the SCCA crown.

Frontier Ford of Niagara Falls, Ontario, attached its name to some fine-running Fords. Wayne Hardwick saw success running this Boss 302 Mustang in Division 3. (Photo Courtesy Rob Potter)

Proving that the apple doesn't fall far from the tree, Randy Ritchey followed in his father's footsteps with this 1969 Mustang, which is shown at the NHRA Winternationals. Capable of running well below the record, Randy held the SS/IA mark as late as mid-1970 with an ET of 11.83 at 117.34 mph. (Photo Courtesy Don Prieto)

The Boss 302 was created by fitting Cleveland heads onto the 302 block, and the Boss Mustang proved to be a killer on the SCCA circuit. Drivers of the four cars in the front of the pack are Parnelli Jones (front on the inside), Peter Revson (behind Jones), George Follmer (on the outside), and Dan Gurney (behind Follmer). (Photo Courtesy Revs Institute/Albert R Bochroch)

First-year Boss 302s were fitted with oversize 2.23 intake valves; later engines were fitted with 2.19 intake valves. The NHRA didn't help the engine out when it immediately refactored it to 325 hp. It did find a life in Pro Stock during the mid-1970s when racers used it to build smaller inch Clevelands.

The Big, Big Boss

When NASCAR disallowed the exotic SOHC 427 from competing against Chrysler's Hemi on the big ovals, Ford went back to the drawing board and returned in 1969 with the Blue Crescent 429. NASCAR rules dictated that at least 500 units had to be sold before being homologated. Although the Torino was Fords go-to car in NASCAR, the Mustang was chosen to carry the Blue Crescent 429. Semon "Bunkie" Knudsen, with his keen eyes on performance, saw room for improvement in Ford's Total Performance program and felt that a unique Mustang fit the bill.

The magic of the Boss 429 was in the aluminum heads. The gargantuan 2.28 intake valves flowed a straight path

The Boss 429 was the fiercest engine Ford ever stuffed between the shock towers of a production-based Mustang. This one resides in the restored **Mr. Speed Inc.** *match race Mustang of Al Joniec.*

Although the Boss 429 Mustang didn't see a lot of initial drag strip success, it became quite the collector piece. Over time, guys such as Dyno Don, Jon Kaase, and Bob Glidden would made the engine much feared on the track. Here, Vern Tinsler (line operations) at Kar-Kraft (in the white shirt on the left) holds the Job #1 sign with pride. (Photo Courtesy Wes Eisenschenk)

to semi-hemispherical combustion chambers. The compression ratio was 10.5:1 while a 735 Holley mounting on an aluminum intake fed the fuel. A forged crank and rods were supported by four-bolt main caps. Sealing the heads to the block were copper O-rings.

Make no mistake, this was a pure race engine detuned to 375 hp so that it may live on the street. Its low-14-second quarter-mile times in stock trim reflected this. The engine was produced for two years only and didn't see much success on the drag strip until the match race Pro Stockers took to the engine in the dying days of the 1970s.

Back with the Funnies

While the door cars were now receiving most of the factory attention, the Funny Cars of notables Gas Ronda, Tommy Grove, and Tasca Ford returned with fac-

tory support. Joining the battle against Chrysler Hemi cars were a handful of standouts that included Dick Loehr, Paul Stefansky, and Jack Chrisman. The Funny Car, gaining in popularity since 1965, had by 1969 surpassed the Top Fuel dragster in fan appeal. To cash in on the popularity, several Top Fuel teams chose to run a car in both categories.

Top Fueler Connie Kalitta, enjoying factory support of his own, surprised many when he debuted a Mustang Funny Car at the season-opening NHRA Winternationals. Connie was having great success in Top Fuel running

For several years beginning in 1969, Connie Kalitta ran a Funny Car alongside his Top Fuel car. Power initially came from a Boss 429 followed by a Cammer and finally, by the end of 1970, a Ramchargers-built Chrysler Hemi. (Photo Courtesy Michael Pottie)

Gas won his share of big meets. He closed the 1969 season by winning the Sears Points Funny Car Championship. Gas was a stand-out with Ford, and a member of their Drag Council going back to the early 1960s. (Photo Courtesy James Handy)

An engineer by trade, Dick Loehr switched back to Ford power in 1969 with this 427 SOHC Mustang. Fellow Michigan company Logghe Stamping built the chassis for the Chapman Performance Products machine. Loehr ran a best ET of 7.35 at 202 mph in 1969, which was his last year in a Funny Car. (Photo Courtesy Michael Pottie)

Tasca's last kick at the can came in 1969, when the Rhode Island dealer fielded this Cammer-powered Super Boss Mustang. Bill Lawton and mechanic Jeff Healey made a great team, but in the end, Tasca was in the business of selling cars, not Funny Cars. (Photo Courtesy Lou Hart)

a Cammer-powered rail going back to 1965, winning multiple national events prior to being lured by the money that tracks were paying to Funny Cars. Kalitta's Mustang ran the gamut from a 429 to an SOHC 427 and, finally, to a Chrysler Hemi.

Junior Brogdon returned in 1969 with a more conventional Phony Pony Mustang Funny Car. The new car ran an early 392 Hemi and was a solid 7-second performer. Junior took a break from racing at the end of the 1970 season. He made a brief return in the mid-1970s to run a Pro Stock Pinto. (Photo Courtesy Lou Hart)

The Return of Mickey Thompson

Mickey Thompson, who originally contracted with Ford in 1964, returned to the fold in 1969 after a five-year hiatus. He ran three Mustangs for the manufacturer: two Cammer-powered Funny Cars, a Mach 1 driven by Dan Ongais, and a Mach II driven by Pat Foster. Both Mustangs featured innovative chassis built by Pat Foster and John Buttera. The cars played a key part in the evolution

Mickey Thompson was a busy man in 1969. He manufactured parts, performed research and development for Ford, and campaigned several drag cars. His Danny Ongais-driven blue Mustang won almost everything in 1969. (Photo Courtesy Don Prieto)

Still unlettered at this point, Mickey Thompson's red Mustang was piloted by Pat Foster. Pat and John Buttera were responsible for building the 121-inch-wheelbase chassis that housed an SOHC 427 engine. (Photo Courtesy Don Prieto)

The year 1969 belonged to Danny Ongais and Mickey Thompson's Mach 1 *SOHC 427-powered Funny Car. Danny went 55-3 through the year, and the only real losses were at the Winternationals, United States Professional Dragsters Championship, and the World Finals. (Photo Courtesy Johnny Kilburg)*

At the expense of Ford, Mickey Thompson got in on the heads-up action in 1969 with this Butch Leal-driven Boss 429 Mustang. The car was prepped by Holman-Moody-Stroppe and recorded a best ET of 10 flat. (Photo Courtesy Brian Kennedy)

Al Joniec was busy in 1969. The Funny Car ran the injected Gas Funny Car circuit for a while, and his Cammer-powered match racer was a feared car in the Northeast. If that didn't keep him busy enough, there was his Mr. Speed Inc. speed shop. (Photo Courtesy Charles Morris)

A Gapp in Funny Car

Outside of the AA/FC category that received most of the attention, there were numerous injected Gas and Fuel Funny Car classes that time seems to have forgotten. AHRA's short-lived Gas Funny Car Circuit saw both Al Joniec and Wayne Gapp competing. Rules were few and straightforward: a maximum 430 ci and a minimum 2,000 pounds. Al purchased Art Malone's 1969 Mustang and ran a few races with an injected SOHC 427. Although the mill (pretty much the same one that powered the *Batcar* into the 8s) made plenty of power, the excessive weight of the fiberglass body made the car too heavy to be competitive.

Before the Pro Stock category, Wayne Gapp found success on the AHRA injected gas Funny Car circuit with his 1969 Mustang. The Mustang is pictured between rounds at Thompson Raceway in Ohio. (Photo Courtesy Todd Wingerter)

I'm sure Wayne Gapp would have liked to have run his 1969 Mustang more than what he did. As well as working as an engineer within Ford's performance program, Wayne also operated his own engine-building business, Performance Engineering. That is, until Ford found that this conflicted with the work he was doing for it. To appease Ford and keep his job, Wayne brought in Jack Roush to handle the day-to-day operations.

Gapp chose to run the Boss 429 in his Mustang and developed his combination as he went along. Seeing that the aftermarket was slow in jumping on the engine, Gapp fabricated several his own parts, including his own fuel injection and drive by using Hilborn parts. When it came to a transmission, Wayne must have been the first to successfully adapt a C-6 to the 429. The Mustang consistently ran in the 8.80s.

The 120-inch-wheelbase Logghe chassis of Gapp's Mustang came from under Pete Gates's old 1966 Comet Funny Car. Rules allowed for a 33-percent engine setback, as opposed to the Fuel Funnies, which were limited to a 25-percent engine setback. The injection was fabricated by Gapp. (Photo Courtesy Todd Wingerter)

of the Funny Car by adopting the narrow Top Fuel style of chassis.

The Cammers mounted solid to the chassis, which went against the sliding mounts commonly used at the time. The only suspension adjustments possible were dialing in the four Koni coilover shocks. Foster's car featured a more flexible chassis with thinner inside-diameter bottom rails and a 5-inch longer wheelbase (121 inches).

Ongais and his Mustang were the year's success story, running away from the competition with a reported 55-3 win-loss record. The Mustang's only real losses came at the Winternationals, the United States Professional Dragsters Championship, and the World Finals. Along with all the wins, Ongais recorded the first 6-second Funny Car run when he drove the Mustang to a 6.96 on September 14 at Kansas City.

Rounding out Thompson's stable was a heads-up Boss 429–powered Mustang driven by Butch Leal. The Mustang was an original Kar-Kraft prototype Mustang that was acid dipped and prepared with the help of Holman-Moody-Stroppe.

They prepared two more heads-up Mustangs for Drag Team members Hubert Platt and Ed Terry. While Platt and Terry chose to run with the proven Cammer, Thompson/Leal stepped up for the manufacturer and went to work testing and developing the new Boss engine in their Mustang. Thompson's right-hand man Fritz Voigt went through the 429, replacing weak springs, installing M/T aluminum rods and pistons, and trialing experimental aluminum heads that featured resized and reshaped ports. A Toploader transmission and Dana rear completed the driveline. Rumors of a stroker crank persisted and was said to help the Mustang record a best ET in the high 9s at 135 mph.

Heads-Up Super Stock

The heads-up Stockers were really grabbing headlines in 1969. Based on minimal rules, the AHRA first introduced a heads-up, no-break-out category in 1968. For all intents and purposes, this was Pro Stock as it is

Al Joniec dropped $4,200 at sponsor Rice & Holman Ford on this Boss 429 Mustang with full intentions of replacing the engine with a Cammer. The match racer doubled as Al's first Pro Stocker in 1970. Although more than holding its own match racing, the Mustang made anything but a memorable appearance at the 1970 NHRA Gatornationals, where the car qualified 16th in the 16-car field with a 10.36 ET. By the time the Summernationals rolled around, Al was in an SOHC Maverick.

Through 1969, one of the nation's most feared Ultra Stock cars was the Wedge-powered Mustang of Sam Auxier Jr. Sam won the heads-up category at the Cars Magazine Meet at Cecil County for the second year in a row. He defeated Grumpy Jenkins the first year and Ronnie Sox the second. (Photo Courtesy Eric English)

known today and was dominated by Camaros, A-Body Mopars, and Mustangs.

Sam Auxier Jr. and Dave Lyall are just two drivers who chose to run Mustangs. Both cars ran the tried-and-true Tunnel Port 427. Both drivers focused most of their attention on running circuit races and AHRA events. At the sanctioning body's Springnationals in Bristol, Tennessee, Dave defeated Grumpy Jenkins's Camaro with what has been reported to be the first legal 9-second run by a Stocker. Dave revved the engine to 8,000 rpm while power shifting to a recorded 9.98 clocking.

Although the ET has been questioned, Dave stated that his Tunnel Port 1967 Fairlane had run 10.0s at three different tracks the previous year.

"In '69, my Mustang was faster and quicker than Ed Terry's or Hubert Platt's SOHC cars and as quick or quicker than Nicholson's SOHC Cougar," Dave said.

Either way you want to slice it, the days of the 9-second Stockers were upon us.

AHRA Ultra Stock rules differed from NHRA, as they allowed things such as flip front ends and no front brakes (as long as you ran a parachute). In 1969, no tunnel-ram style of intake was available for the Wedge, so many went with one or two carburetor spacers that gave more of a ram effect. (Photo Courtesy Eric English)

A Ford man through and through, Dave Lyall had his two Mustangs competing at the 1969 Super Stock Nationals. Pictured are his Boss 429 heads-up Going Thing *Mustang and his original lightweight 1968* Cobra Jet *Mustang. The heads-up car ran legal 9.90 ETs. Here, Dave thrashes to repair a busted rear. (Photo Courtesy Michael Pottie)*

Ford Drag Team Leads in Super Stock

In 1969, Ford looked to further promote its performance line by creating the Ford Drag Team. It followed in a similar vein as Chrysler's drag clinic program, though Ford referred to its program as seminars, focusing on performance and safety. Two drag teams were created, a West Coast team consisting of Ed Terry and Dick Wood, and an East Coast team consisting of Hubert Platt and Randy Payne. Ed and Hubert were considered the team leads.

Each team visited dealerships during the week, drawing crowds that averaged 500 people. The teams promoted Ford's muscle parts, set up drag clubs, and visited local tracks on the weekend for some match race or Super Stock action. The first Drag Team seminar took place at Foulger Ford on January 14.

The team cars consisted of a non–Ram Air (Q-code) Cobra Jet Mustang and an R-code Cobra Jet Torino. While Platt ran his Mustang with a trusted C-6 automatic in SS/IA, Terry's Mustang ran a stick in SS/I. Platt's 1968 Torino was updated and joined the team as a 1969 model driven by Payne in SS/J. Wood had himself a new Torino that he campaigned in SS/JA. The cars each ran in alternate classes to ensure they would never meet in a class final. The three new cars were sent to Holman-Moody-Stroppe, where they received pretty much the same upgrades as the original six 1968 Cobra Jet Mustangs.

The first race for the cars was the 1969 NHRA Winternationals where, along with the Mustangs of Barrie Poole, Geno Redd, and Roger Caster, both Platt and Payne won their class.

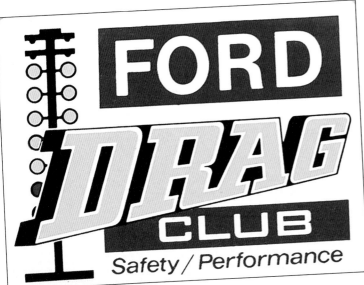

The Ford Drag Club was "the going thing," and serious business. It organized five major drag races around Southern California in 1970. The last one was held at Fremont in September and sponsored by Hayward Ford.

The C-750 car carriers supplied to the drag teams were first class and fully loaded. The metallic blue and pearl white matched the colors on the drag cars. The side stripes on the Mustang were lifted from the Boss 302 parts bin.

The Ford Drag Team West Coast consisted of Ed Terry and Dick Wood, who were both proven winners. The Torino ran SS/JA, while the Mustang ran SS/I. Ed Terry won the Division 7 points title in 1969 with the Mustang.

Hubert Platt, seen here at Dallas, dominated his class with his Mustang. Platt won the 1969 AHRA U.S. Open at Rockingham in September, defeating the Don Carlton-driven Road Runner of Sox & Martin in the final. (Photo Courtesy Dale Schafer)

Here, at Sears Point International Raceway, Ed Terry gets the jump on the Penetration II Dodge Dart. Ed held the SS/H ET record with an 11.42. In March 1970, Dick Wood took a turn behind the wheel and gave the Mustang a win in AHRA GT-1 class during a race at Lions Drag Strip. The GT classes were dominated by Camaros, so the win no doubt felt pretty good. (Photo Courtesy James Handy)

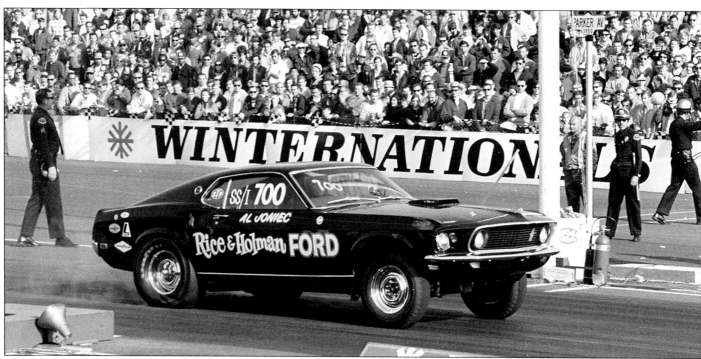

Ford put Al Joniec into this Rice & Holman Ford Cobra Jet Mustang at the Winternationals in 1969 in hopes of a repeat victory. In a warm-up race to the Winters, Al defeated Grumpy Jenkins's Camaro with a record ET of 11 seconds flat. At the Winternationals, Al lasted until the third round of eliminations before falling to eventual winner Don Grotheer. (Photo Courtesy Al Joniec)

Rowland Heights, California, resident Geno Redd's Cobra Jet was an AHRA and NHRA class winner and record holder. Geno won his class at both the 1969 and 1970 NHRA Winternationals. Sadly, Geno lost his life a year later in an on-track incident while testing a Pro Stock 'Cuda. (Photo Courtesy Lou Hart)

This Cobra Jet Mustang was owned by singer Vick Demone and pro golfer Ken Venturi. Driven by Rick Schrameck, the Mustang recorded mid-11 times thanks to a Bob Spears–built 428. (Photo Courtesy James Handy)

For the Mustangs, the remainder of the season unfolded with equal results. At the next Springnationals, John Elliott in his Cobra Jet Mustang won SS/GA, while Ed Terry won SS/I, J.C. Downing won SS/G, Bob Glidden won SS/JA, and Platt won SS/IA again. At Indy on Labor Day weekend, John Elliott won SS/F, Ken McLellan won SS/G, Barrie Poole took SS/H, Dave Moran won SS/FA, Bill Allie won SS/GA, and Platt once again took SS/IA honors.

Changes to the Drag Team came late in the season, as the Torinos of Randy Payne and Dick Wood were retired, and Platt and Ed Terry debuted match-race Holman-Moody-Stroppe-prepped Cammer-powered Mustangs. The 1969 Drag Team Mustangs were given a face lift at the end of the season, taking on the new 1970 Mustang front clip and taillights and panel. In possibly the Super Stock Mustang's last race, Platt won SS/HA class at the NHRA Nationals.

Meanwhile, in Stock . . .

While the Mustangs, old and new, held their own in Super Stock, national event wins in Stock were a little tougher to come by. It wasn't from a lack of trying though, as buddying drag racers across the nation and Canada came out in force. Their efforts paid off in local wins, but it appeared that the more serious racers avoided Stock, which seemed to cater to the Chevys. Change was coming though, albeit slowly.

Eddie Clarke bought his 1969 Cobra Jet Mustang new from Wood Motors in Fredericton, New Brunswick, Canada. The car was a heavy hitter on the East Coast and was always an E/S class threat with low-12-second ETs through 1970. (Photo Courtesy Bob Boudreau)

There was room for every brand of Mustang in drag racing. The West Chester, Pennsylvania–based team of Cross and Sandoe ran its 2-barrel 289-powered 1965 GT coupe down in J/Stock.

John Bushwalter from San Gabriel, California, ran D/SA at the 1969 NHRA Winternationals. Mid-12-second ETs made the Mustang competitive, but no class winner was decided. (Photo Courtesy Don Prieto)

Tasca Super Boss

Tasca's Super Boss carried a stunning Paul Shedlik paint job and wheels to match. Tasca had ideas on building a better Boss that never panned out. (Photo Courtesy Tasca Ford)

Bob Tasca Sr., who in 1962 coined the term "Race on Sunday, Sell on Monday," knew what it took to sell cars. When Tasca retired, the *Super Boss* Mustang Funny Car was the car that reaffirmed Tasca's commitment to performance.

The *Super Boss* debuted in 1969 and was a showpiece for a stillborn street package that the Rhode Island dealer considered selling. Powering the Mustang was an aluminum Can-Am Boss measuring 494 ci. Backing the estimated 700-hp mill was a C-6 transmission.

The Mustang was the ultimate promotion piece. Running on street tires, the car was match raced against anyone who dared to step up with a street car. If you were lucky enough to beat the Mustang, which ran 11-second times, you were paid a cool $1,000. No doubt there were few who collected. With open pipes and slicks in place, Bill Lawton squeezed 9.50s at more than 140 mph from the Mustang prior to retiring the car in 1971.

Even against the toughest competition, the Tasca Super Boss got it done, thanks to the aluminum Boss 494 under the hood. It's believed that 50 of these aluminum blocks were produced. (Photo Courtesy Tasca Ford)

Dyno Don Goes Full-On Ford

Dyno Don Nicholson, who was voted Funny Car driver of the year in 1968 while driving his Mercury Cougar, returned to the door cars in 1969. He campaigned his last Mercury, an SOHC-powered heads-up Cougar briefly in early 1969 before purchasing the SOHC-powered Mustang of Jerry Harvey.

Hubert Platt had a short stint in the Mustang during 1968, driving it long enough to set the A/MP class record at Indy with a 10.75. Don purchased the Mustang late in 1968 as a runner and continued to race it in Modified Production as well as money-making match racing. The car required little tweaking by Don and his crew chief, Earl Wade. Although, Wade recalled, "The car took a week to clean off all the dirt and grease and oil. Harvey didn't take real [good] care of it."

The King of the Funny Car, Don Nicholson, had his fill of the floppers by the end of 1968. In 1969, he took over ownership of the former Jerry Harvey Mustang and won Street Eliminator with it at the NHRA Springnationals. (Photo Courtesy Michael Pottie)

Running A/MP at the NHRA Springnationals, Don earned his first NHRA national event category win since the 1962 NHRA Winternationals by taking Street Eliminator.

The category was a mixed bag consisting of cars from Gas, Sports Production, Street Roadsters, and Modified Production. Don battled his way to a final round appearance against the C&W Motor Parts–sponsored B/SR of Ralph Smiderle by defeating the Gassers of Mitch Mitchell and the *Mr. Crude* Anglia of Canadian Ralph Hope. He got a bye run in the third round before facing the D/SP Corvette of Bo Laws in the fourth. Bo had the slower car and was given the handicap start.

The Cammer Mustang had no problem catching the Corvette and overpowered the big-block Chevy, with a 10.57 at 112.07 mph. In the final, Don let it all hang out and took the win with a record ET of 10.49 at 120.96 while Smiderle trailed with a 10.649 at 127.47. Don followed the win in September by taking A/MP class at Indy, where he lowered the class record with a 10.40 time. In match-race trim, the Mustang ran a best of 9.87 at 135 mph before Don made the move to a Pro Stock Maverick.

Ohio George Continues his Dominance

Ohio George, the undisputed king of the Supercharged Gassers, retained the title with the debut of his 1969 Mustang. Ford provided him with a prototype Mach 1 to lay up a fiberglass shell, which he placed over a 1933 Willys chassis. Supporting the car was a ladder-bar rear suspension and a tube axle up front. The suspension featured coilover shocks at all four corners, which allowed George to fine tune to specific track conditions. Initially, the Mustang was powered by a blown SOHC 427 producing a reported 1,200 hp, which was backed by a beefed C-6 transmission and 9-inch rear end. The car dominated at its Indy debut, winning Super Eliminator by defeating the Hemi-powered AA/Altered of Ron Ellis in the final. In the process, George set the AA/GS record with an 8.59 at 164.23 mph.

George stuck with the combination until 1971, when he switched to a Boss 429. Not satisfied with the run-of-the-mill 6-71 blower setup, George took it to

The shell of the Mr. Gasket-sponsored Gasser is all fiberglass and was formed using a preproduction 1969 Mustang. George's Mustang debuted running AA/GS, but by the time the car was retired, it was labeled by the NHRA as a BB/Altered Turbo. (Photo Courtesy Bob Martin)

The interior of the Mustang screams 1969. The floor tin remained flawless as George placed mats before hopping in the car. The candy-striped seats, like the exterior, features heavy metal flake. (Photo Courtesy Jerry Heasley)

Ohio George initially ran a blown SOHC 427 in his Mustang before making the switch to twin turbos late in 1970. With the support of Ford Engineer Danny Jones, George dipped into the manufacturer's Indy parts bin to come up with the twin Schwitzer turbos. The unique setup had each turbo feeding two cylinders on opposing sides of the engine. The fuel delivery system was by Bendix, and ignition was by Mallory. The compression ratio was in the neighborhood of 7.0:1. (Photo Courtesy Michael Pottie)

the next level and installed twin Schwitzer Turbochargers. Although Ford had pulled its racing support by this point, George enjoyed back-door assistance from Ford's Indy expert, Danny Jones. The pair relied heavily upon the manufacturer's defunct Indy program for turbo parts and technology.

In a previous interview, George had stated that it took a couple of years to work out the bugs, but once the car was sorted, it cranked out times of 8.40 at 175 mph. As turbo technology was lagging (no pun intended) at the time, the trick was to kill some of the top end and try to compensate for the turbo lag. The guys downsized the fuel nozzles and modified the stock Boss heads, taking the 2.28 intake valves down to approximately half the size.

"We killed 400 to 600 top-end hp in an attempt to overcome the initial lag," George said. "Each turbo was putting out over 30 pounds of boost, and we were beating everyone."

Due to the car's killer mid-range and top end, they just drove around cars that were quicker off the line.

A highlight of George's career was winning the NHRA Gatornationals in 1973 and repeating the victory in 1974. The results didn't seem to make the NHRA very happy. Not fully understanding turbo technology, the association felt that George was holding back on power

and penalized him for it by forcing him to run with a handicap. Eventually, George's combination was outlawed by the NHRA. Basically, the NHRA let him know that the car was no longer welcome, and he retired it at the end of 1975.

The Cars of Modified Eliminator

Modified Eliminator was a category for dual-purpose, street and strip, American-built cars. The most popular

Popular West Coast racer Dan Holmes and his A/MP 1965 Mustang were right in the thick of action here at the 1969 NHRA Winternationals. For the San Bruno, California-based Mustang, 10.60 ETs were common. (Photo Courtesy Don Prieto)

classes in this category were Gas and Modified Production. It was a pretty cool category that allowed any modification as long as the car remained "streetable." You could run any engine in any body, no matter the make or brand. It definitely made for some interesting combos: Mustangs with Wedge engines, Hemi engines and, gulp, Chevy engines. Anything went.

1970: Game Changers and Bandits Steal the Show

Appearance-wise, the big change in the 1970 Mustang came in the form of a revised front clip that had the car reverting to single headlights. Other changes included the filling of the side scoops and a change in side stripes. Gone was the GT, while the Mach 1 option gave you grille-mounted driving lights. The 4-speed received a Hurst shifter and T-handle but kept the factory shift rods. The high-horsepower 351 Cleveland received a bump in compression, going to 11.0:1, which pushed the horsepower rating to 300.

Stone, Woods, and Bones Balogh campaigned Swindler A *Chrysler Hemi-powered Shelby Mustang in 1969. The Mustang and its superior aerodynamics helped change the face of the Gas category. (Photo Courtesy Don Prieto)*

It was a rare site to see a Mustang running A/Gas. This northern California-based Mustang ran ETs of 10 seconds flat this day at Fremont. Standard A/G goods included a setback engine, injectors, a one-piece fiberglass front end, and a straight axle. (Photo Courtesy James Handy)

With the NHRA factoring the Boss 429 engine to 410 hp in 1970, you didn't see many of them in class action. Pat Mahnken's Mustang gave it a good shot and saw some success. (Photo Courtesy Lou Hart)

Jack Mezzomo was a popular Northwest racer. In 1970, his D/MP 1966 Cobrastang *Mustang ran a best ET of 10.88 at 124 mph, thanks to a transplanted Boss 302. For several years, Jack operated Pro Speed & Custom Engines out of Burnaby, British Columbia, Canada. His customers covered the spectrum of motorsports. (Photo Courtesy Murray Chambers)*

Tragedy at the AHRA Winternationals

In the world of Funny Car, Ford was in a pickle. Parts for the SOHC 427 were drying up, and the Boss 429 had yet to see the kind of development needed to make it a genuine threat. The situation fueled the continued decline in Ford-powered Funny Cars.

At the AHRA Winternationals, Tommy Grove showed them all that the Cammer could still be counted on. His Mustang showed all the Chrysler-powered cars the way home. Tommy saved the best for last when he defeated the Jake Johnson–driven Hemi-powered *Blue Max* in the final with a 7.54 ET at 195.65 mph.

A tragic event at the same race saw the career of Gas Ronda come to an end when his Cammer let loose. The explosion caused the transmission to come apart, spewing burning fluid onto Gas. He survived but received third-degree burns over much of his body. He spent a year recovering from the burns, going through many surgeries and grafts.

If there were any upside to the incident, immediately after, the sanctioning bodies mandated that all Funny Cars be

With Tasca retiring from drag racing early in 1970, it left only two competitive all-Ford Mustang Funny Cars on the East Coast: Paul Stefansky's Super Stang and Jerry Caminito's Holeshot. Jerry, a popular Ford racer going back to the mid-1960s, ran an SOHC backed by a Bob Rose C-6 transmission mounted in a Logghe chassis. Best ETs were in the 6.90s at 214 mph. (Photo Courtesy Bob Snyder)

Jack Chrisman briefly ran this Mustang in 1970 as he developed his rear-engine Mustang Funny Car. Jack was a Ford man through and through and was responsible for some of drag's most interesting innovations. (Photo Courtesy Lou Hart)

Seen here at the 1970 Super Stock Nationals is the highly competitive Mustang of Tommy Grove. Tommy stuck to running the SOHC 427 in the Logghe chassis car until the supply of high-nickel blocks ran out. Tommy lost the Mustang in a trailer fire. (Photo Courtesy Bob Snyder)

Buddy Winward (crew chief) and Joe Jacono (driver) purchased the ex-Tasca Mustang in 1970. Brief Encounter *seems like an appropriate name for the car. The Mustang was burnt to the ground by a friend's irate girlfriend shortly after its debut. (Photo Courtesy Michael Pottie)*

fitted with fire-suppression systems. The Mustang was rebuilt and campaigned by the team of Amis Saterlee and Mike Pohl with minimal success.

In retirement, Gas worked for Foulger Ford in West Covina, California. It's said that sales of performance parts at Foulger increased by 1,000 percent when Ronda came on board.

Mickey Thompson

Mickey Thompson had a full slate in 1970, running up to five cars (three Mustangs) through the season, and all with Ford power.

Johnny Wright, driving a white Boss 429-powered Mustang, gave Mickey his first big win of the year when he won a major Funny Car bash at Irwindale in January, defeating the AMC Javelin of Clyde Morgan with a 7.65 at 193.12 mph. Last year's Funny Car standout Danny Ongais gave Thompson his last national event win with Ford when he wheeled his Cammer-powered Mustang to a win at the AHRA Gran-Am race in March, defeating the Hemi 'Cuda of Don Prudhomme on a flag start. The Christmas tree had been damaged in the previous round by flying shrapnel after Don Garlits's Top Fuel dragster exploded its transmission.

Mickey Thompson was truly one of the sport's more innovative thinkers and designers. From hemi heads for Pontiacs and Fords to his aluminum pistons, rods, and finally tires.

The wheels in his head were once again turning in 1970, when he and Nye Frank came up with the monocoque Mustang Funny Car. The unique design experiment combined the body

The Mickey Thompson's Mach 1 *Mustang driven by Dan Ongais received a face lift in 1970 in the form of a new body. Chrysler Hemi–powered cars made things a lot tougher for Ongais in 1970, and he failed to come close to his 1969 results. (Photo Courtesy Lou Hart)*

Borrowing from his Indy Car experience, Mickey Thompson came up with the monocoque Mustang Funny Car in 1970. The full potential of the car was never realized, as development died in the spring of 1970. Mickey fielded five different cars in 1970. (Photo Courtesy James Handy)

Corpus Christi–based Bob Veselka purchased Dick Loehr's Stampede Mustang and saw some success of his own. A Cammer powered the Mustang to 7.30 ETs in 1970. (Photo Courtesy James Handy)

and an inner-tube structure as one, which was similar to an aircraft or Indy car style. There was no chassis, and all the main components tied to the inner structure. To access the inners, the body flipped up along the belt line. The Mustang weighed 1,850 pounds, which was about 300 pounds less than Mickey's conventional Mustang Funny Car. The best ET for the Boss 429-powered car was a 7.40 at 196 mph. Development on the Mustang died in the spring of 1970 as factory support disappeared and the car's performance to that point was nowhere near expectations.

Pro Stock and the Maverick?

When it came to running Pro Stock, the Maverick had two advantages over the Mustang: 1) it weighed a few hundred pounds less than a comparative Mustang, and 2) its overall dimensions were smaller than the Mustang; so, at speed, it pushed less air. The advantage proved itself at the NHRA Winternationals where Pro Stock made its debut. Three Cammer-powered Mavericks qualified; seven Mustangs tried and failed.

The Ford Drag Team started the season running Pro Stock with its heads-up Mustangs. The cars were stuck in the low- to mid-10-second bracket as they proved to be too heavy to compete against the lighter cars in the upper echelon of the class.

Super Stock & Drag Illustrated magazine did an article on Platt's Mustang in February 1970, where 9-second quarter-mile times had been predicted. The two teams' heads-up Mustangs began life as showroom models before being sent to Holman-Moody-Stroppe for their reworking. The SOHC 427 that filled the engine bays featured the standard go-fast goodies of the day: twin Holley 740-cfm carbs drew air from Ram Air tubes, which were fed through the inner headlight openings; 0.640-lift Crane cams; Mickey Thompson rods; and ForgedTrue pistons that squeezed out 12.5:1 compression. Backing the 427 was a close-ratio Toploader and a 9-inch rear end containing 4.86 gears. Helping to bring the weight down was a bare-bones interior; fiberglass fenders, hood, doors, trunk lid; and lightweight side windows.

Jack Chrisman, the man some call the father of Funny Car, campaigned this gorgeous Mustang in 1969. The paint and body was crafted by the famed designer Paul Shedlik, and the chassis was completed by Dick Fletcher. In 1969, the SOHC 427 powering the Funny Cars produced nearly 1,400 hp. (Photo Courtesy Don Prieto)

With less weight and smaller dimensions than the Mustang, the Maverick was the Ford racer's preference in Pro Stock during the category's first two years. None was better than Dyno Don's Cammer car. (Photo Courtesy Michael Pottie)

Holman-Moody-Stroppe prepped this Pro Stock Mustang for Ed Terry using a bare-bones Foulger Ford-supplied car. Terry's Mustang made its first runs late in 1969 and produced ETs in the low 10s. (Photo Courtesy Lou Hart)

By the Nationals in September, where only two Mustangs were entered, a change in direction saw the Drag Team members all in Holman-Moody-Stroppe-built Cammer-powered Mavericks. Joining the Drag Team early in 1970 was Dick Loehr, who himself was competing with a Pro Stock Maverick. Dick came on board just as talk of Ford ending its involvement in racing had begun. By the end of the season, it was official: Ford was done. A changing environment saw funds once allotted to racing activities now directed to emissions controls.

Drag Club Alumni

Ford pulling the plug on racing spelled the end of the drag teams and seminar program. In total, the teams had established drag clubs at 143 dealerships across the U.S. and Canada that counted 16,500 card-carrying members. These clubs maintained a grassroots presence on local tracks and should be recognized for doing their part in bringing buying customers into Ford showrooms.

Hubert Platt was always in the thick of the action. His 1969 Mustang Pro Stocker began life as an R-code 428 Cobra Jet Mustang. Powered by an SOHC 427, Hubert squeezed ETs in the high-9s at 145 mph out of the Mustang. (Photo Courtesy georgiashaker.com)

Several dealers offered support to the drag racers, forming clubs and cutting prices to members on performance parts. Foulger Ford of Monrovia, California, took this van to tracks and displayed their goodies. (Photo Courtesy Pat Mahnken Family Archives)

A Cammer fills the engine bay of Hubert Platt's Pro Stock Mustang. Carburetor spacers under the Holleys helped to make up for the lack of an available hi-rise independent runner intake manifold. (Photo Courtesy Allen Platt)

The Ford Drag Team seminars were well received and usually consisted of overflowing crowds. Here, Drag Team Boss Hubert Platt dishes out tips and tricks while answering questions. (Photo Courtesy Allen Platt)

as wins were proving to be too costly for the dealer.

The Wilson Ford Drag Club was such a success that it continued to operate into the 1980s, giving rise to several future Stock and Super Stock class winners and record holders: Tom Stafford, Jeff Powers, Marcel Cloutier, Steve Steele, Don Lutz, Larry Saugstad, Dave Budgett, Don Rea, and "Pogo" Joe Burke, among others.

At the close of the decade, Ford led all manufacturers in car sales, and no doubt sales of performance cars had increased from the meager 8 percent of the market that the manufacturer had held just a few short years earlier.

Wilson Ford

Wilson Ford in Huntington Beach, California, is just one example of the success the seminars had. Dick Wilson loved his drag racers and gave them his full support. No doubt, he lost a little coin to the racers as he matched their winnings dollar for dollar. This changed over time

Bob Brown and Crew Chief Bob Lavery's SS/FA CJ Mustang was capable of sub-record 11.60 ETs in 1970. As an engine builder, Bob had his hands on many winning eastern Mustangs. (Photo Courtesy Michael Pottie)

Bill Ireland enjoyed the support of Ford through the mid-1960s but ran as an independent after 1968. Here, in 1970, he faces Dave Wren for about the millionth time, battling it out in Super Stock at the old Mission Raceway in British Columbia, Canada. (Photo Courtesy Murray Chambers)

The FastBacks team began when a group of dedicated Ford employees got together and decided to go drag racing. With Bill Allis behind the wheel, the team was SS/GA class winner at Indy in 1970. ETs in the 11.70s were common for the SportsRoof. (Photo Courtesy Bob Martin)

Ford Canada Clinic

In 1970, Ford Canada created a drag team seminar program of its own. The team consisted of four cars, each prepared by Barrie Poole: a G/SA 429 Cobra Jet Cyclone, an H/S 428 Cobra Jet Cougar, an SS/HA Cobra Jet Mustang, and a Pro Stock SOHC Mustang. Hauling the cars from coast to coast was their just-as-familiar *Titanic* hauler. This thing was so large that routes had to be planned before hitting the road to avoid overpasses.

The three Stock and Super Stock cars were owned by Ford, while the Pro Stock Mustang belonged to Mike Wood. The Mustang began life as a 1969 Boss 429 Kar-Kraft test car that was converted to appear as a 1970 model. The drivers were Scott Wilson, who drove both of the Mustangs, and Vic Beleny, who drove the Cyclone and the Cougar. Later, former record-holder Louie Rivait took over the driving chores on the 428 Mustang and Bruce Fitzgibbon took the wheel of the Cougar. The Canadian Drag Team was short lived and died when Ford cut its racing budget.

The Ford Canada Performance Clinic followed along a similar vein as the U.S. seminars. Although not as successful on the track as the U.S. Drag Team, the Canadian effort proved to be just as effective in getting buyers into the showrooms.

Unlike Ford in the U.S., which eventually had three drag teams, Canada had just one that crisscrossed the country. This 428 Mustang ran Super Stock. (Photo Courtesy Rob Potter)

The car hauler used by Canada's performance clinic, dubbed the Titanic, was an impressive site. The rig was so tall that routes had to be planned in advance to avoid overpasses. (Photo Courtesy Rob Potter)

Those Dreaded Border Bandits

The Cobra Jet Mustangs owned the Super Stock F, G, and H classes and the automatic counterparts, winning all six classes at the Winternationals, Springnationals, and Indy Nationals in 1970.

No one was winning rounds like the Canadian-based drag team of Sandy Elliott. The team consisted of Barrie Poole driving an SS/H 1969 Mustang coupe and John Elliott in an SS/FA 1968 fastback. Poole was responsible for building the Cobra Jet engines and prepping the two cars. By the end of 1970, he was preparing cars for dealers as far away as Winnipeg and Halifax.

"By that time, we were also doing the cylinder heads for probably 75 percent of the Cobra Jet racers in Canada," Barrie said.

Barrie and John earned their nickname, the Border Bandits, due to their ability to swoop down into the U.S. from their home in Chatham, Ontario, and rob their American counterparts of wins before heading home. Although the team had been around since 1966 when it debuted a competitive D/SA Comet, the team first drew national attention in 1969 when John (driving a 427-equipped 1967 Comet) won his class at the NHRA Winternationals. Barrie, for his efforts, won the first *Popular Hot Rodding* meet and played runner-up to Ronnie Sox at the Springnationals behind the wheel of the team's 1968 Cobra Jet Mustang. Barrie kick started the 1970 season by winning Super Stock at the NHRA Winternationals, turning in a record-setting ET of 11.26. This was a first for the team, as no other Canadian had ever won an NHRA national event. He followed with a runner-up finish at the next Gatornationals.

Not to be outdone, teammate John Elliott won the team its second national event of the year by defeating the Mopar of Bob Lambeck at the Springnationals.

Barrie and John faced each other in the final round at the 1971 *Popular Hot Rodding* race with Barrie grabbing his second win of the prestigious event. Closing the season, Barrie won the Division 3 points championship (for the second year in a row) with John coming in a close second. Adding to their conquests, in 1971, Barrie and his SS/H Mustang won Super Stock Eliminator at the Winternationals by defeating the 1965 Dodge of Jim Clark with an 11.28. John, for his efforts, won SS/F class. Later in the year, the pair repeated class wins at Indy. Come 1972,

The Border Bandits, Barrie Poole and John Elliott, ran both 4-speed and automatic classes with their two Mustangs. The pair had a friendly agreement with Ken McLellan (Cobrastang) that each would stick to their own class.

Super Stock eliminations at the 1970 World Finals in Dallas saw Barrie Poole in the far lane fall to teammate John Elliott. For the period of 1969 through 1971, few could match the record performance of these two. (Photo Courtesy Steve Reyes)

Border Bandit John Elliott (shown driving) was division champ in 1968 with a 427 Comet. In 1969, he took over the team's fastback when Poole moved into the 1969 coupe.

The Cobra Jet coupe of Barrie Poole was a multi-time record holder and class winner. In 1969, Barrie won the Division 3 points title and set the SS/J record with an ET of 11.76 at 118.42 mph. He slipped in a C-6 and set the SS/JA record with an ET of 12.05. Running SS/H here at the 1971 Winternationals, Barrie's combination had an estimated 335 hp. (Photo Courtesy James Handy)

Barrie focused his attention on a new Pro Stock Comet while John stepped back from racing.

Canadian Heads

Benefitting several Ford-supported Cobra Jet racers, including Poole (who received his worn heads prior to the 1971 Winternationals), were the better-breathing Canadian heads.

As told by Bruce Sizemore and posted on the 428cobrajet.org website, he developed the heads in clandestine. The heads were produced in August 1969 and first appeared in use at the NHRA Nationals. Bruce was

A Stark Hickey ringer, this one belongs to Ed Shumate and is at the 1970 Super Stock Nationals running against the Hemi Dart of Ron Mancini. Renowned engine builder Billy Williams prepared the Jet Set Cobra Jet. (Photo Courtesy Michael Mihalko)

taking a risk, as the heads were developed without the knowledge of Emil Loeffler, the head of Ford's racing program.

With the competition breathing down Ford's neck, Bruce set out to produce a new intake-port core for the foundry that flowed considerably more CFM than the original 428 head. In the 428cobrajet.org story, Bruce stated that he began working with Allen Buckmaster of Ford's Scientific Research lab. This is where experimental engine development work was carried out. Bruce had 14 sets cast at Dearborn Iron Foundry over a quiet weekend.

Machining was done by Paramount Boring and Machine, a company that did most of Ford's NASCAR prototype work. Paramount finished the heads except for the all-important valve seat and CC minimum

The *Gunfighter*

You're forgiven if you mistook Gary Coe's Oregon-based 1969 Mustang for a Funny Car. Gary, a longtime Ford proponent, may best be remembered for his D/Altered altered wheelbase 1957 Ford, or the Pro Stock Pinto wagon he raced in the mid-1970s, a car he drove to defeat Warren Johnson in the first round of eliminations at the 1977 NHRA Fallnationals.

The *Gunfighter* Mustang fell between those two cars and ran C/Altered with an injected Wedge engine. It featured a home-fabricated chassis and leaf spring rear suspension. After crashing the car, Gary replaced the body with a 1971 Mercury Comet.

There are times when a black-and-white photo just doesn't do a car justice. This is one of them. Gary Coe ran this Mustang in the Altered class. (Photo Courtesy Murray Chambers)

The *Lawman* Mustangs

In 1970, Al Eckstrand teamed with Ford in presenting the military forces overseas with a drag seminar. A half-dozen cars were built, but the king of them all was this Boss 429-powered Mustang. The car survives and was restored by Anghel Restorations. (Photo Courtesy lawmanmustang.com)

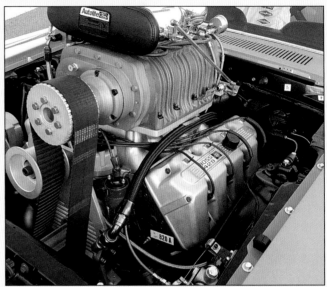

Just like the original, a Hampton blower and Hilborn injection top the radical Boss 429. Dyno results showed 1,000 hp and 800 ft-lbs of torque. The block is numbers-matching to the car. (Photo Courtesy lawmanmustang.com)

Some readers may remember or have read previously of Al Eckstrand and his half-dozen *Lawman* Mustangs. For those who haven't, here's the story.

Al, a drag racer at heart (he won the 1964 Winternationals driving for the Ramchargers) and a corporate Chrysler lawyer, approached Ford with the idea of creating a drag team that would visit U.S. troops overseas. Al wasn't new at this, as he had originally put a similar program together back in 1966 and called it the American Commando Drag Team, which featured a Hemi Charger.

With Ford approval and backing from Goodyear, B&M, Hooker, and Hurst, among others, Al and mechanic Jack Watson took the cars on tour through Europe, Southeast Asia, and the Pacific during 1970 and 1971. Similar to the drag teams at home, Al's program focused on performance as well as safety. The added punch that really gave the troops a boost was the improvised drag races that were held.

The Mustangs were shipped directly from Dearborn to Roy Steffey Enterprises in Fairhaven, Michigan, where the modifications were performed. All of the cars were Cobra Jet powered with the exception of the original Kar-Kraft Boss 429 car.

Two of these Hampton-blown Mustangs were built, the first one was lost when it was crushed by a container on a loading dock in Vietnam. The 429 reportedly produced 1,000 hp and was backed by a B&M-prepped C-6 transmission. It has been said that upward of a quarter-million servicemen took in the seminars, which helped earn Al an honorary citation from the U.S. Department of Defense.

resurfacing work. For that, Bruce approached Domenic Garofali, a trusted Ford Experimental Garage employee. Dom did the valve job at his house in Dearborn Heights with lightweight valvetrain parts supplied by Holman-Moody. There, he also checked chamber volume for compliance with NHRA's 68-cc minimum specification, playing it safe by going with 69 cc.

Dom delivered 11 sets to Paul Harvey Ford in Indianapolis where the selected cars were already torn down waiting for installation. Jerry Harvey was not slated to get a set for his SS/E Mustang, but Paul Harvey insisted. The heads were already spoken for, so at Emil's request, Dom flew back to Detroit and finished another set. Completed, he wrapped them up and caught a flight back to Indy. Interesting enough, Jerry Harvey's Mustang was the only class winner (after Dave Lyall was disqualified for heads) at the event. Once the heads were discovered by the NHRA, it added a 10-hp factor.

CHAPTER 4

1971-1973

NEW STYLING, SAME GO-FAST GOODNESS

With its fourth redesign, the Mustang once again grew in proportion, picking up 2 inches in length and width and another 200 pounds in weight. For the first time, the Mustang saw a growth in wheelbase, going from 108 to 109. Although it was bigger overall, the new Mustang looked fast standing still, thanks in large part to its long hood, short deck design, and the new fastback SportsRoof, which laid the rear window at a 14-degree angle. Ford carried the bodystyle through 1973 with appearance changes limited to the grille and striping. The real changes came under the hood.

We were now entering an era where the emphasis wasn't so much on performance. The onslaught of higher insurance rates, low-grade fuel, and government intervention combined to kill the performance market. Dark days were fast approaching but not before Ford and the Mustang got in a few final licks.

TOP: *Galpin Ford sponsored a string of cars, including Paul Lesser's 1971 Mustang Stocker. Ford counted heavily on dealers and clubs to draw attention to the manufacturer's performance offerings. (Photo Courtesy Lou Hart)*

1971: Carrying on the Winning Ways

The top-of-the-line performance offering for the Mustang in 1971 was the Super Cobra Jet 429. Horsepower was pegged at a peak 375 while torque came in at an earth-turning 450 ft-lbs. In stock trim, you were looking at a solid mid-13-second bruiser. The NHRA did Ford no favor when it factored the engine to 425 hp. This made the combination uncompetitive and ensured anyone choosing to run the engine was going to be fighting an uphill battle.

Former Top Stock World Champ Bud Shellenberger (1965) wheeled this Super Cobra Jet Mustang for Maryland's Norris Ford. Bud drove the Mustang to a runner-up finish in SS/E at Indy in 1971. The bare-bones Mustang recorded ETs in the 10.90s.

Next in line behind the 429 was the Boss 351, which was rated at 330 hp and came stuffed with 11.0:1 compression, a solid-lift cam, four-bolt mains, and an Autolite 750-cfm carb. Ram Air was standard on the Cobra Jet and Boss 351 equipped cars and optional down through the base 351. The Mach 1 now carried a top option 351 with 10.7:1 compression, a Holley 780 carb and a 285-hp rating.

Factory Involvement Disappears

When it comes to Ford's involvement in drag racing, it's easy to look back and think about what could have been, had the company stuck with it in 1971; it's even easier when you see the paperwork. An internal memo from the Performance Events Department dated November 4, 1970, called for six Mustangs to be built for Super Stock competition. Powering the cars would have been specially prepared 385 series 429 engines. Those who were to receive the Mustangs were Bob Glidden, Chuck Foulger, Bob Frensley, Rusty Gillis, Tom Schumacher, and Nate Cohen.

In addition, there were to be parts deals made for a group of Stock class competitors: Richard Charbonneau, Dave Markle, Jack Worrell, and Nate Cohen. Not to be left out, support would be given to eight The Lincoln-Mercury dealers. With emphasis changing from performance to economy, all factory deals, Stock, and Super Stock were quashed before the 1971 season even started. Of course, there were still several dealerships willing to help out the racers.

When support for the racers ended in 1970, all of Ford's performance engineers were moved into emissions. A meeting was held at Holman-Moody-Stroppe the Sunday after the Winternationals that was attended by Drag Race Manager Bruce Sizemore, Emil Loeffler, and a few other Ford reps. The meeting, which was attended by approximately 200 racers, was held to announce that all factory support would end. Tony Rainero was one of those who attended the meeting, and he recalled that when they were asked for a show of hands as to who would continue to race without factory support, only 15 to 20 people raised their hands. It is unknown how other Ford racers were notified that support would not continue.

Shortly after, while visiting Detroit, Rainero received a call from the skunkworks to come and load up his truck and trailer with all the parts he could use. Whether he was the only one who received such a call is unknown. It is known that Buddy Baker purchased a boatload of parts, including all the good aluminum CJ pistons.

Stocks and Super Stocks

Although factory involvement had ceased, there were plenty of competent souls to ensure that the Mustang, and other fine Ford products, remained in the winner's circle. At the Winternationals, five Cobra Jet Mustangs

Eddie Spencer ordered this Super Cobra Jet coupe new from Ken Cole Ford in Xenia, Ohio, with drag racing in mind. The Mustang was torn down the day it arrived. Eddie and partner Ron Stevens (with some help from George Montgomery) went through the engine. Eddie raced the car for a few years with great success, and is shown here in 1971. (Photo Courtesy Bob Martin)

The Ulrey brothers' (Mike is pictured here in 1971) winnings go back to the 1960s, when they had an AA/S Ford and a B/S Ford that were both very successful in and around the Midwest. The AA/S car held the national top speed record for a while in 1965. Their string of Mustangs (and a Fairlane) won class at numerous events and set multiple records. (Photo Courtesy Bob Martin)

won their respective classes. Four won class at the next Springnationals, and six won at Indy. In addition to the wins was the fact that Cobra Jet Mustangs held records in six classes for most of the 1971 season. Although the 351-powered 1971 model Mustangs were slow to catch on, when they did, they proved to be a worthy adversary.

The Coal Digger *Shafts the Competition*

Just a little over 1,800 Mustang buyers chose the 429 when optioning out their 1971 Mustang. Most leaned toward the Boss 351 or the 351-powered Mach 1.

Don Bowles, who hailed from Madisonville, Kentucky, seems to have been the first to see success with the new Mustang. Don found happiness with his 1971 model through the mid-1970s, initially running the car in its original Boss setup (330 hp) before reworking the car as a more class favorable 285-hp (factored by the NHRA to 325 hp) Mach 1.

The car was showroom fresh when Don went to work tearing it down in preparation for its life on the drag strip. Don had a close relationship with Jack Roush and counted on Gapp & Roush to help prepare the Cleveland mills. Don ran the car through 1976 in SS/I, J, and K, and won his class at the NHRA Sportsnationals in 1974, 1975, and 1976. Additional class wins came at Indy in 1975, and in 1976 when he battled his way to the final before falling to the Dodge Challenger of Dave Boertman.

Don sold the Mustang as an SS/J record holder (10.97 at 123.11 mph) to Harold Stout who continued setting records and winning with the car. In 1981, the Mustang again made it to the finals at Indy where history repeating itself saw the Mustang again come up short, this time against the Fairlane of Ray Paquet.

Don Bowles of Madisonville, Kentucky, was runner-up at Indy in 1976, running a 10.88 ET on an 11.23 index. The Mustang was an original Boss 351 car but ran as a more class-favorable Mach 1. (Photo Courtesy Bill Truby)

In 1977, Don Bowles's Coal Digger found a new home with the team of Stout and Bruce. The Mustang again made it to the finals at the U.S. Nationals in 1981 under Stout and Wilson before falling to the Fairlane of Ray Paquet. (Photo Courtesy Don Wilson)

The World Champ Cobrastang

The year began with Barrie Poole winning the Winternationals and finished with Friona, Texas, wheat farmer Ken McLellan and his *Cobrastang* winning the World Finals. Ken, a natural competitor, was born with a mechanical aptitude like no other. He became serious about drag racing around 1965 and ran the gamut from Stockers to Experimental Stock cars. His *Cobrastang* was one of Ford's dollar cars and was picked up from Foulger Ford after getting a workover from Holman-Moody-Stroppe. An original raven black Mach 1, Ken had the local painter Bob Fulks lay on the custom red paint.

Just as they had with their previous cars, Ken and Joe did all the modifications and maintenance on the Mustang themselves at the farm, and they put the farm

Ken McLellan was the 1970 Division 4 Super Stock points champ and 1971 world champ. The **Cobrastang** first set the SS/G record in 1969 and held on to it well into 1973, which was a year after Ken retired the car. (Photo Courtesy Tom Ordway)

equipment to use. To prepare an engine prior to rebuild, Ken ran it on his irrigation pump to break it in before he took it apart to rebuild it for the Mustang.

While Joe tended the 1,000-or-so acres, Ken headed to regional tracks with the Mustang. In 1970, their efforts won them the Division 4 title. In 1971, their dedication paid off with a World Championship title win. In the Super Stock final, Ken defeated Canadian Dick Panter's SS/DA Hemi 'Cuda with an 11.75 at 117.95 mph. Ken recalled that he never lost class in the car, excluding the 1969 Springnationals, which he threw, giving the class win to Ed Terry. It was a smart move, as Ken's previous low ET allowed him back into the program and gave Ford an extra car in eliminations.

Ken raced the Mustang through to the 1972 World Finals, where he lost to Val Hedworth after breaking an axle on the line. After the World Finals, Ken was talking with Bob Glidden about the cost of racing Super Stock. There was no real money to be made and both felt that you either had to go all in or get out of it.

At the next race (the Supernationals), Glidden debuted his Pro Stock Pinto while Ken, with kids and a farm needing attention, chose to retire. He packed up the *Cobrastang* and ramp truck with a few extra parts and sold the works to Rusty Gillis.

Rusty Gillis:
Proof that Timing Is Everything

Rusty Gillis attended the Nationals in 1969 as a spectator and ended up crewing for Hubert Platt. Little did he realize that he'd be helping out for the next couple of months.

Ken McLellan's 1969 Mustang was a $1 car from Ford. The company supplied him with all the parts and pieces he needed prior to the company pulling out of racing in 1970. In one of his rare AHRA appearances, Ken won his class at the 1970 AHRA Winternationals. Ken didn't make use of a line lock on the Mustang. Instead, he held the brake pedal down with a stick. He short-shifted the Toploader and was in second gear before the Christmas tree. (Photo Courtesy Dale Schafer)

By no means your run-of-the-mill 428, this one belongs to Rusty Gillis. Sitting atop the PI intake manifold and 1-inch spacer is a stock 735 carburetor with 70 primary jets and 80 secondary jets with a 105 power valve. Inners include a Crane cam with 0.612 lift that is retarded a couple of degrees. Polished LeMans rods with SPS bolts hung 0.025-over Forged True flat-top pistons with stainless-steel Dykes rings. (Photo Courtesy Rusty Gillis)

Helping Randy Gillis's Mustang off the line was an A1 converter with 4,200 stall speed, 5.14 gears, and 29.5-inch-tall Firestones. Rusty left the line at a high idle and shifted at 7,000 rpm, going through the lights at around 7,200. (Photo Courtesy Rusty Gillis)

In 1970, the NHRA changed the Super Stock weight breaks, adding half a pound to each class. The Ram Air engine that Rusty Gillis ran had flat-top pistons, lightweight valves, and was rated by the NHRA at 360 hp. The class minimum weight for SS/GA was 3,240 pounds. The shipping weight of the Mach 1 was 3,303 pounds, whereas the base 1969 fastback had weighed 3,272 pounds. So, Rusty removed the Mach 1 interior to bring the weight closer to the low end of the break. (Photo courtesy Rusty Gillis)

The relationship between the two proved to be mutually beneficial. In November, Rusty purchased Platt's 1968 Winternationals runner-up Mustang. He prepped the Mustang and had it ready in time for the 1970 Winternationals. It was a good showing for Rusty, who thought he had won SS/FA class, but upon teardown, it was discovered by tech that the deck height was out by 0.002 inch. Rusty made up for it in 1971, when he returned to win class cleanly and set the class record.

In July 1971, Rusty purchased a 1969 Mustang from Platt (and a pair of Canadian heads) and swapped the drivetrain from the 1968 Mustang into the 1969. The car had been previously used by Ford as one of the test mules for the Boss 302 model. In 1972, Rusty returned to the Winternationals, where he won SS/GA class. Rusty had done some tire testing for Firestone in late 1971, replacing his 11.5-inch tires with softer 9-inch tires and picked up 0.2 seconds in doing so. He won his class at the Winternationals on the 9-inch tires recording a best of 11.28.

The 428 powering the Mustang carried 0.025-over ForgedTrue pistons, polished Lemans rods, and a Crane flat-tappet cam. The C-6 housed an 8-inch A-1 convertor, reverse-pattern valve body, and Hurst dual-gate shifter that Rusty moved throught the gates at 7,000 rpm. Out back was a Detroit locker that carried 5:14 gears. When weighed the Mustang came in at 3,145 pounds, 127 pounds under its ship weight, so in went a spare tire, jack, and a full tank of gas. Eventually, the Mustang ran the quarter mile in the 11s.

After building a new drivetrain for the sidelined 1968 Mustang Rusty entered both cars at the 1973 Winternationals. Joe Varde drove the 1968 Mustang to a runner-up finish in SS/FA, while Rusty himself drove the 1969 Mustang to a runner-up finish in SS/GA. Rusty said the cars were slowed by issues they had with the C-6 transmissions.

"I had someone who had a successful transmission shop build them," Rusty said. "He tried something that worked in a Mopar but not a C-6."

At the next Gatornationals, Rusty debuted the *Cobrastang* that he purchased from Ken McLellan. He set the SS/GA record at Suffolk in April with an 11.26, short shifting at 6,500 rpm. The following day, he ran an 11.13 at 122.95 mph. Rusty retired from class racing in October of 1973.

Tony Rainero: Stark Hickey Mustangs See Success in the 1970s

Tony Rainero campaigned his Mustang with success through 1974, running both SS/H and SS/HA. Behind the Cobra Jet, Tony ran either a Toploader or a C-6 transmission that housed a Winters 5500 stall convertor. Helping to transfer weight to the rear were 6-cylinder coil springs and Koni shocks. Tony's relationship with Ford goes back to the mid-1960s, when he worked on the company's turbine program.

Anthony (Tony) Rainero's Stark Hickey–sponsored Mustang has a history similar to the 1969 Mustang that Hubert Platt sold to Rusty Gillis. This Mustang was ordered by Ford Engineering for use as a mechanical prototype test vehicle. After it was constructed in August 1968 at the Dearborn Assembly Plant, it was taken to the Automotive Assembly Division (AAD) Pilot Plant in Allen Park, Michigan, for conversion to a 1970 model Prototype test car.

Initially, the 1969 body panels and components were replaced with 1970 "production intent" body parts along with new power brakes, up-sized spindles, a hand-built (serialized) steering gear, and other components requested by the Engineering Activities that would be using the car for testing. In February or March 1969, many of the interior components were updated, but the 1969 instrument panel and steering column were retained. By August 1969, the Mustang had lived out its life as a test vehicle.

The Special Vehicles Group determined which prototype test vehicles could be sold (for $1) to Ford Team Racers. As mentioned previously, Hubert Platt got one and Tony Rainero got another. When Tony picked up the car, the early Boss 302 engine and transmission were absent. A "Crib Requestion" form came with the car's paperwork so Tony began withdrawing all the necessary parts from the DX Crib in the Experimental Garage (X-Garage) where his cousin Domenic Garofali worked as a mechanic.

Once Tony got the car running using spare parts from his 1968 lightweight Mustang, he put the car on a trailer and drove it to Holman-Moody-Stroppe in Long Beach,

California, for further upgrades. There, Wally Cartwright built the 428 SCJ engine, and a striking Burgundy pearlescent paint job (that Tony was able to pick from multiple renderings done by Ford's Styling Center) was applied.

Ford Special Vehicles paid Holman-Moody-Stroppe for the engine and the mechanical upgrades, but Stark Hickey Ford, Tony's sponsoring dealer, got invoiced for the $3,000 paint job. The dealer balked at paying for the expensive finish until seeing the car a few weeks later at the Winternationals in January 1970.

Tony had great success with the Mustang through 1974, running both SS/H and SS/HA. He won his class at the 1971 Summernationals and the Winternationals in 1972. The SCJ featured all the modifications you would expect in an early-1970s Super Stock mill and then some, and it moved the car to sub-record low-11-second times.

Starting at the top of the engine, a variety of intakes were tried by Tony, including a Shelby intake and a Sidewinder, each topped by a slightly modified 735 Holley. Tony had a good friend at Holley who polished the bores and then re-dyed them (Holley were the only guys who had the correct dye) to look stock. There's no doubt that the carburetor flowed more than 735.

Internal modifications to the engine included TRW pistons, a 0.651-lift General Kinetics flat-tappet camshaft, and a crank reworked by Moldex. Tony's Mustang generally ran 40 to 42 degrees advance, and by way of a dash-mounted cable, he could retard the timing a few degrees on the top end.

Frank Lundgren and Tony Rainero were promised by Ford a 1968 Boss 302 Mustang, but when production was delayed, they were handed the keys to this Cobra Jet Mustang. Although it was capable of 11.30 ETs, Frank was unable to pull off a class win here at the 1969 Winternationals. (Photo Courtesy William Bozgan)

Stark Hickey paid the $3,000 bill for the custom paint, which consisted of pearls over royal maroon and gold-leaf lettering in a design created by Ford's styling group. (Photo Courtesy Lyle Barwick)

One of the more elaborate modifications made to the Mustang was a viscous clutch from a fan that mounted between the harmonic balancer and pulley. This was an idea and a part that was literally stolen from under Chrysler's nose. With the clutch placed in this location, it not only allowed the fan to free-wheel but also the water pump and alternator. According to Tony, on a Cobra Jet engine, this freed up 5 to 6 hp.

Tony got wind of the clutch from a sponsor who told him it was only available to Mopar racers. A little misleading trickery on Tony's part saw the clutch fall into his hands. In 1971, at the Gatornationals, he was tech'd in with the part in place. The next day, the NHRA decided it was not going to let any of the Chrysler guys use it because they didn't make it available to everyone. The kicker was that Tony had already tech'd in with it, so he was allowed to run with it. It was the only time he ran it, as he was told by officials not to show up with it again.

Tony, like his competitors, worked to cure the oiling issues that were hereditary to the 428. His cure to the problem was no doubt similar to what many racers were doing: baffling, restricting oil flow to the top end, redirecting oil, increasing pump volume and pressure, etc. Tony ran his motors around 65 pounds of oil pressure, while other builders often ran much higher. Another thing Tony figured out quickly was that the clearances Ford was saying to use on the FEs for racing were too loose. He ran them tighter and had discussions with Wally Cartwright at Holman-Moody-Stroppe, who agreed with what he was doing.

Another issue related to the 428-equipped Mustangs was traction. Super Stock rules of the day limited racers to track bars or ladder bars, and whatever tire fit the stock wheel well up to 11 inches in width. Barrie Poole may have been the first to recognize the advantage of adjustable ladder bars by fabricating his own. According to Barrie, he never changed his bars once they were set. Tony went further by slipping a pair of Mopar Super Stock springs under his 4.86-gear-equipped 9-inch rear.

With the help of Tom Smith (Wolverine Chassis), they made some changes to the front mount point and re-positioned the center hole. The springs ended up sticking 6 to 8 inches out the back of the Mustang. Tom solved that issue by cutting off the excess and rerolling the rear spring eye. Just like that, he had a Mustang that launched like no other.

Tony Rainero used head-machining plates on the Cleveland after discovering the heads moved around when torqued to a block. Tony stated that the plates looked like a 3½- or 4-inch chunk of the upper end of a block. The heads were torqued to spec to the plate before all work was performed. Tony's CJ was a non-Ram Air, dished-piston, heavy-valve engine that ran SS/H and was rated by the NHRA at 345 hp. (Photo Courtesy Lyle Barwick)

He later backed half the Mustang and did some bracket racing with it during the late 1970s. Rusty has retained the *Cobrastang* all these years, and in 2005, he started the long process of restoring the car to the way it was raced in 1972.

Stock

In Stock, the Mustang fought an uphill battle against early Chevys that seemed to have been built to suit each class. Tom Schumacher helped to right the ship.

Tom and his 1969 Cobra Jet Mustang were a prime example of what to expect from the Ford racer in the following decade. Tom had been kicking butt in Stock with his 1967 427 Fairlane before making the switch to SS/G with his Mustang in 1970. Having nothing but problems, he reconfigured the Mustang and ran Stock with it in 1971. The Mustang set the F/S class record in July with

an 11.96 at 115.83 mph and won class at Indy on Labor Day weekend.

"You couldn't hurt the engine in Stock, as it only turned 6,000 rpm," Tom said in an interview with the author.

Stock rules limiting modifications helped Tom's combination. He ran with stainless-steel Dykes top ring, no second ring, and a standard Perfect Circle oil ring. A Crane blueprinted cam actuated the valves while different-length pushrods allowed the 428 to turn a few more RPM.

Pro Stock

As impressive looking as the 1971–1973 Mustang appeared, due to its size, few considered the car serious Pro Stock material. Looking back, there were only two (three if you count Larry Sengstack's rebodied Bob Glidden 1970 Mustang) that were known to have competed: Sam Auxier Jr. and the car of the Polaris Drag Team.

Sam Auxier Jr.

Limited by Pro Stock rules of the day, the two took similar but different approaches when it came to building their cars. Sam, a well-established racer who enjoyed the benefits of Ford support chose the 1971 Mustang body for three reasons. First, the engine bay was wide enough to fit the Cammer. Second, the longer wheelbase ensured a better handling car. Sam was just stepping out of a Pro Stock Maverick that was giving him the "heebie-Jeebies" at speed. Third, the Mustang was lighter than most people thought.

Tom Schumacher built this Cobra Jet Mustang in 1970 to run SS/G. It was an expensive year, as Tom had a tough time keeping the bottom end together and getting the car to perform. He returned to Stock in 1971, where he had no issues and picked up a class win at Indy.

In late 1968, Mickey Bogden of Windsor, Ontario, bought his CJ Mustang new from Essex Farmer, a local Ford dealer. With the help of a Barrie Poole-built 428 the Mustang consistently ran to the F/SA record. (Photo Courtesy Carol Bogden)

Sam bought his Mustang as a body in white from the New Jersey assembly plant. *Body in white* is a term used to describe a bare body shell received from a manufacturer.

"We were going to acid dip the car like Chrysler did, but we measured the steel and realized it was 20 percent thinner than the Chrysler cars already," Sam said. "We figured that if we dipped it, there would have been nothing left of the car."

Sam's Mustang went together with the helping hand of fabricator Chick DeNinno. A roll cage was added

Few saw hope for the new Mustang in Pro Stock, but Sam Auxier Jr. showed them what the car could do. Seen here at the Super Stock Nationals in 1971, Sam's Mustang clipped off a reported best ET of 9.50 at 138 mph. (Photo Courtesy Bob Snyder)

Old Pro Stocks never die; they just become killer Modified Eliminator cars. Rick Auxier took over his brother Sam's 1971 Mustang, replaced the Cammer with a Wedge, and made it a top-running Gas class car. (Photo Courtesy Sam Auxier Jr.)

to the car that not only offered full driver protection but also tied the front and rear sub-frames together. To gain additional working room, the shock towers were pushed out 3 inches per side. To lighten the car, fiberglass panels were used for the fenders, hood, and decklid. In place of disk brakes up front, Sam ran with 9-inch Maverick drums. A Diest drag chute was incorporated just in case.

The stock-cubic-inch Cammer was fitted with all the go-fast goods of the day, including a tunnel ram manifold that Vic Edebrock fabricated for Sam by using a Hilborn injection base. A Toploader transmission was backed by a Dana rear, which carried 5:12 gears and was supported by

28-inch track bars. Although major event victory escaped the Mustang, the car reportedly ran a best of 9.50 at 145 mph before Sam retired it in 1973.

"That Mustang was one of my best," Sam said. "The car was really light, and was deceiving. The weight balance was better than the '69 Mustang. We raced two times a week, match races and circuit races, but we opened up Maryland Hi Performance Sales, so we stayed a little closer to home, racing up and down the coast between North Carolina and New Jersey."

Polaris Drag Team

Andy Plym and his Polaris Drag Team started their build with a showroom-fresh Grabber Blue Mustang equipped with a 6-cylinder. Andy had partnered with Larry Mihalek, who was a Ford employee and a coordinator for the Ford Drag Team clubs. The pair came together back in 1968 and campaigned a Mustang before friend Jack Roush suggested a 1969 Cobra Jet coupe to run SS/HA. When the decision was made to step up to Pro Stock in 1971, it was Larry who suggested the Mustang body. It seems to be that Larry was told by a friend in engineering that the Mustang had superior aerodynamics when compared to the Maverick.

They started the Mustang build by stripping the car and sending the body to California to be acid dipped. Unlike Auxier, this pair felt the metal could go a little thinner. Upon its return, it headed to Logghe for chassis modifications and the installation of a six-point roll cage. Under the hood went a Gapp & Roush–prepped Boss 429. For a transmission, the team bypassed the commonly used Toploader and instead went with a clutch-activated

The Polaris Drag Team *Mustang made its debut at Indy in 1971. However, it was unable to qualify with a best ET of 10.02 due to new-car issues. A matching Super Stock car and tow rig had the team winning Best Appearing Crew honors. (Photo Courtesy Mecum Auctions)*

The high-port Boss 429 was built by the team of Gapp & Roush and features the best goodies of the day: Holley, Edelbrock, and Crane. Note the relocated shock towers. (Photo Courtesy Mecum Auctions)

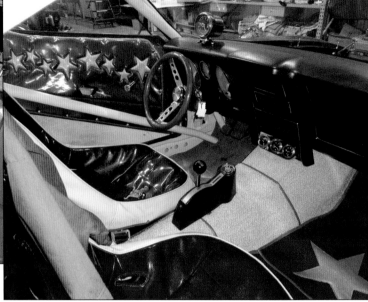

The far-out paint scheme carried over into the interior. Jerry Baker was hired to man the controls. The transmission was a C-6 that incorporated a clutch to get it off the line. (Photo Courtesy Mecum Auctions)

From any angle, the Polaris Drag Team Mustang looks sharp. The Mustang started out as a plain-Jane, Grabber Blue SportsRoof powered by a low-end 6-cylinder. The car was stripped and acid dipped before being sent to Logghe for chassis and tin work. (Photo Courtesy Mecum Auctions)

C-6. Backing that was a Dana 60 rear with 4:88 gears.

The Mustang debuted at Indy in 1971 where its eye-popping red, white, and blue paint, the matching C-series tow rig, Super Stock Mustang, and appropriately dressed crew won them Best Appearing Crew honors. The stars-and-stripes paint scheme carried over into the interior as well as the headers with one being painted blue and the other red.

It's a shame that the Mustang's performance never lived up to Plym's expectations. The car failed to qualify at Indy, where 10-flat times just didn't make the 9.50 field. The team campaigned the Mustang into 1973 with no major victories.

Pro Stock was going through so many changes early on, and the Mustangs of the Polaris team and Sam Auxier were being left behind. New rules for 1972 saw the small-cubic-inch compact cars taking over the category. Their lower weight and higher rev capabilities surpassed the capabilities of the Cammer-powered Mustangs as well as the Mavericks. While Auxier kept pace with the competition by building a Cleveland-powered Pinto for 1973, the Polaris team folded. Plym's parents, who had been bank rolling the endeavor and seeing little return, pulled the plug.

Funny Car

The year 1971 was the last year in which the Ford-powered Mustangs were a genuine threat in Funny Car. Tommy Grove, Jack Chrisman, Paul Stefansky, and Mickey Thompson were just a few who battled on in the face of Chrysler's Hemi onslaught. Grove, who continued to set track records and win his share of rounds with 6.80 times in the neighborhood of 215 mph, was hoping back and forth between Ford and Chrysler power by the end

By 1971, Paul Stefansky's Super Stang Mustang was one of the few competitive Ford-powered Mustangs running. Doug Nash prepped the Cammer, which rode on a Logghe chassis. The chassis was previously found under the Hatton-Stefansky 1966 Mustang Funny Car. Paul ran the 1969 Shedlik body into 1971 before going to the new Mustang bodystyle.

Success came to Tommy Grove due to his ability to draw maximum power from the Cammer consistently. When good Cammer parts dried up in the early 1970s, Tommy moved to Chrysler power. (Photo Courtesy Michael Pottie)

Tommy Grove ran his Logghe Mustang into the early 1970s, alternating with a Chevy Vega body and swapping the Boss for a Cammer and even a Chrysler Hemi. Tommy Grove made a living match racing right up until his retirement in 1977. (Photo Courtesy Fred Von Sholly)

of the season.

Mickey Thompson's stable of Funny Cars in 1971 consisted of a traditional Mustang, an independent-front-suspension Maverick, and a titanium-chassis Pinto. Initially, all of them were powered by the Boss 429. With Ford pulling support in 1970, Mickey saw no reason on continuing to spend his own dime to develop the 429. He ran the engine into the summer before making the switch to a Hemi. Henry Harrison drove the Mustang at Indy in 1971 and recorded a blistering 6.54 qualifying pass before being hampered by mechanical ills.

Jack Chrisman ran his 1970 Mustang into the spring of 1971 before debuting a unique 1971 Mustang that featured a rear-mounted SOHC that was mounted sideways. Multiple gears and a chain transmitted the power to the wheels. The car never got beyond the experimental stage before Jack sold it to Roy Mehus. Roy had no better luck with his *Drag Patrol* before selling it to John Force. This was Force's first Funny Car, which he named *Night Stalker*.

Mickey Thompson stuck with Ford power as long as possible, but with no factory support, good parts dried up. By July 1971, Thompson had replaced his Boss 429 with a Chrysler Hemi. Here at the 1971 NHRA Winternationals, Henry Harrison is driving. (Photo Courtesy James Handy)

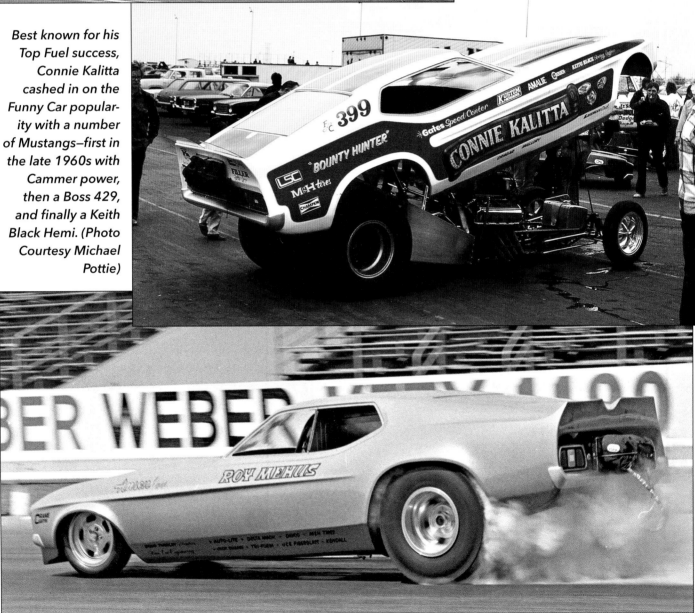

Best known for his Top Fuel success, Connie Kalitta cashed in on the Funny Car popularity with a number of Mustangs—first in the late 1960s with Cammer power, then a Boss 429, and finally a Keith Black Hemi. (Photo Courtesy Michael Pottie)

In 1971, Jack Chrisman built this unique Mustang that featured a rear-mounted Cammer turned sideways. A multitude of gears and a chain transmitted the power to the wheels. Jack never really sorted out the bugs and in 1972 sold the car to Roy Mehus. Roy did no better. The Dragway Patrol was sold to John Force, who set out on his own with his brother, Louie Force, who was in charge of tuning and maintenance. (Photo Courtesy Lou Hart)

In conjunction with his Top Fuel cars, the King of the Northwest, Jerry Ruth, ran a number of Mustang Funny Cars through the mid-1970s. Jerry and his Mustangs won three Division 6 Funny Car crowns. (Photo Courtesy Michael Pottie)

The 1971-1973 Mustang bodystyle was a popular choice in Funny Car; it's a shame that most of them were running Chrysler power. In 1971, Shirley Muldowney made the move from Top Gas dragster to Funny Car when she purchased this Hemi-powered Mustang from Connie Kalitta. She became the first female to win a Funny Car title when she defeated Kalitta at the IHRA Southern Nationals in July 1971. (Photo Courtesy Todd Wingerter)

Veteran drag racer Mike Van Sant is shown at the 1971 Supernationals. Mike borrowed or leased the famed "Stone, Woods & Cooke name" to draw more race dates. It's a shame that the Mustang Funny Car ran a Chrysler mill.

Bill Leavitt's Quickie Too Mustang was the first Funny Car to break the 6.50-second barrier. Leavitt did the deed when he recorded an ET of 6.48 at Lions Drag Strip on December 4, 1971. The time wasn't recognized as a class record, though, as Lions was not a certified track. Powering the Mustang was an early 392 Hemi. In 1975, Leavitt rebodied the car as a Mustang II. (Photo Courtesy Michael Pottie)

The San Antonio-based Brand X Mustang of Cecil Lankford and Dave Sien was a genuine crowd pleaser. A Ramchargers-built Hemi ensured that the Mustang was always in the running. (Photo Courtesy Michael Pottie)

He should have called it *Nightmare*, as that's pretty much what the ill-handling car turned out to be.

Although the Cammer and Boss 429 were on their last gasp in Funny Car, the Mustang proved to be one of the most popular body choices through 1973. Funny Cars were looking a little funnier, as sanctioning body rules now allowed for a minimal body size. Rules read that bodies had to be within 10 percent of the original length and could be as narrow as 65 inches across the wheel openings. The rules also allowed for a 2-inch top chop.

Shirley Muldowney made the move from Top Gas to Funny Car with the purchase of a 1971 Mustang from Connie Kalitta. Shirley earned her first national event victory with the Mustang when she defeated the Mustang of Kalitta at the IHRA Southern Nationals in July 1971.

Shortly after Shirley's marriage to Jack Muldowney ended, she found solace with Kalitta. She adopted the name the *Bounty Huntress* and ran in tandem with Kalitta's similarly painted *Bounty Hunter*. The pair ran the Mustangs with success before moving into Top Fuel.

"Animal" Al Marshall took the wheel of Dale Creasy's Tyrant Mustang in 1971 and won the Division 2 title that year. He repeated the victory in 1972 as well. Along with being regular winners at Coca-Cola Cavalcade of Stars events, the pair was runner-up to Don Schumacher at the 1972 NHRA Grandnationals. The Mustang was campaigned through 1973, traveling coast to coast and winning its share of battles. (Photo Courtesy Michael Pottie)

Bud Richter and Gary Bolger originally teamed in the mid-1960s to run a Chevy Funny Car. In 1971, the pair won the prestigious Popular Hot Rodding meet at Martin, Michigan, defeating Richard Tharp and the Blue Max Mustang in the final. (Photo Courtesy Michael Pottie)

Eventually, Shirley won 18 national events and 3 world titles. Kalitta, who had been racing since the late 1950s, won his first national event in 1967 behind the wheel of an SOHC-powered Top Fueler when he won the AHRA Winternationals. In total, Connie accumulated 14 national event wins.

The Funny Car was in such demand by 1971 that it was drawing equal billing to the Top Fuel cars. A few of those who had a little more disposable cash ran both categories, including Kalitta, Chris "the Greek" Karamesines (who ran a Barracuda alongside his Top Fuel ride before switching to a 1971 Mustang), and Jerry Ruth. Ruth had been dubbed the King of the Northwest due to his record-running Top Fuel. Jerry won the Division 6 title something like five years running. In 1971, he debuted a Pay 'n Pak–sponsored 1971 Mustang Funny Car. He switched to a Mustang II Funny Car in 1977 with Lee Beard behind the wheel before cutting his program back to just the one Top Fuel car. In total, Jerry and his Mustangs won three division titles.

Modified Eliminator

Although it was one of the more popular categories through the 1960s and 1970s, Modified Eliminator (formerly called Street Eliminator) didn't see a lot of Mustangs competing. What didn't help the Cobra Jets and Clevelands was their limited RPM capabilities. This category was dominated by stroked, high-revving Chevys—as high as 10,000-plus rpm.

Further hampering the Cobra Jets and Clevelands was the rule that stated stock production heads must be used. Even so, the few Mustangs that competed in Modified

Although the Modified ranks seemed to be covered by the Chevys, Dick Jackson and his B/MP Mustang regularly took them on with success, turning 10.50 ETs in 1971. Mike Ulrey, usually found in a Super Stock Mustang, could often be found behind the wheel. (Photo Courtesy Bob Martin)

Lexington, Kentucky–based Sherrill Huff ran his injected E/Gas Mustang out of Shively Speed Sport. Sherrill was an avid supporter of the Sportsman categories. In 1988, he purchased Ohio Valley Raceway. In 1971, the Mustang ran competitive 11.20 ETs. (Photo Courtesy Bob Martin)

The IHRA had its own style of Modified cars, and the Penner brothers were game for the competition. The Oklahoma-based Mustang, which is shown in 1971, ran a tunnel-rammed Boss 429. (Photo Courtesy Steve Reyes)

Eliminator usually held their own, running on the record, copping class on occasion, and winning division meets.

1972: Against the Odds

A combination of high insurance rates and a changing attitude toward how we treated mother earth brought on the death of the muscle car. Gone from the Mustang option list in 1972 were all the 429 engines. The top performance engine was now the 351 Cleveland, which was rated at a net (rear wheel) 266 hp.

The Mustang remained a strong performer in Stock and Super Stock but had all but disappeared from Pro Stock with less than a handful of cars in contention. In Funny Car, there were no more competitive Ford-powered Mustangs competing. The Chrysler 392 and 426 Hemis that now dominated the class were joined by the aluminum 417-ci Hemi derivative produced by Ed Donovan.

Funny Car

It's questionable as to whether there was ever a better-looking Funny Car than the 1971 through 1973 Mustang. A combination of the SportsRoof design and NHRA rules, which allowed for down-sized bodies, made the Mustang the perfect candidate for cheating the wind. By 1972, the Mustang seemed to be the racer's choice with an easy dozen being campaigned.

For the Mustang, highlights of the season included major victories for Dave Condit and the L.A. Hooker crew who earned the popular Coca-Cola Cavalcade of Stars Funny Car championship, Richard Tharp in Harry

Quite possibly the most successful Mustang of the early 1970s was the Richard Tharp–driven **Blue Max** of Harry Schmidt. The Mustang won a handful of IHRA national events into 1973. (Photo Courtesy Ed Aigner)

A busy man during the early 1970s, Dwane Ong ran his mid-engine dragster and drove Ray Gallagher's Trader Ray Mustang, which is seen here at Indy in 1972. (Photo Courtesy Ed Aigner)

The Cleveland-based Golden Nugget of Ron Potter saw competition with all three sanctioning bodies. In 1972, the Nugget won the National Dragster Open at Columbus. (Photo Courtesy Michael Pottie)

Schmidt's *Blue Max* dominating at the Orange County International Raceway (OCIR) Manufacturers meet, and Larry Fullerton winning the NHRA World Finals.

L.A. Hooker

Dave Condit, another graduate from the Top Fuel ranks had teamed with the Beaver brothers to drive their rail in 1969. They made the move to Funny Car in 1970 after purchasing Nelson Carter's *Super Chief* Charger. The team match raced the wheels off the car all through the Midwest and headed to Southern California in the winter to bash it out. A Maverick followed the Charger, which was followed by the renowned Mustang.

The team joined with Ben Christ's Coca-Cola Cavalcade of Stars Funny Car circuit in 1971. In 1972, the team won the cavalcade points title on the strength of consistent driving and mid-6-second times. In a previous interview published by the NHRA, Gene Beaver stated

With Dave Condit behind the wheel, the Beaver brothers' (Gene and Richard) L.A. Hooker was the Coca-Cola Cavalcade of Stars series champion in 1972. Formed in 1970, the team members went their own ways in 1974. (Photo Courtesy Michael Pottie)

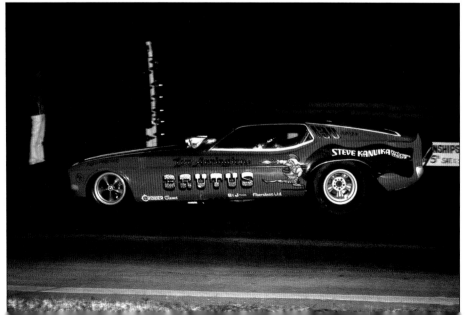

that they won 22 of the 39 cavalcade races that season and were probably runner-up in the remaining races. The 1973 season proved to be a bust for the team who decided to take a break in 1974.

It's the Real Thing

Formed in 1969, the Coca-Cola Cavalcade of Stars was the brainchild of track operator and promoter Ben Christ. The series was created to sustain the smaller tracks that couldn't afford to bring in the big-name racers.

"As a track operator, I was aware of some of the problems that the smaller plants [tracks] faced," Ben said in a 1990s *National Dragster* interview. "Funny Cars were the hottest racing property in the late 1960s, but because the appearance money was high for the good cars, $1,500 to $2,000, a small track could only afford to book one or two. However, [I wondered] what would happen if someone offered you an eight-car show of nationally known cars for half the price? The deal was that the track would pick up half the tab and Coca-Cola got the other half."

The circuit worked (and worked well) through 1976. An added bonus was that the cavalcade helped gain star billing for some of the lesser-known teams that otherwise may never have been recognized.

The Trojan Horse: World Champ

Larry Fullerton and partner Kevin Doheny earned their NHRA Funny Car world title the hard way. Fullerton had not had a national event final-round appearance all season and was a good tenth behind final-round opponent Jake Johnston, who was wheeling Gene Snow's Dodge Charger. Although Fullerton had previously recorded a best of 6.42, he was stuck in the 6.60s at the World Finals. Meanwhile, Johnston had been ripping off 6.50s all weekend.

Lew Arrington hung with the Coca-Cola set, but by 1972, he had left the circuit. His Mustang is seen here in 1973. He lost the car at Epping that year and returned in 1974 with an unorthodox mid-engine Camaro labeled Hell-Fire. (Photo Courtesy Michael Pottie)

The days of Larry Fullerton and partner Kevin Doheny racing Mustang Funny Cars dated back to the late 1960s. None were more successful than their World Champion Mustang pictured here. "Lil" John Buttera provided the chassis, while an Ed Pink Hemi provided the power. (Photo Courtesy Michael Pottie)

Well, as they say, races are won and lost on the starting line. Johnston's Hemi dropped a cylinder on the run and could do nothing but watch as Fullerton went on to win with a day's best of 6.58. The World Finals win was a beneficial one for Ford Motor Company as well, as it was its first Funny Car world title. Although Fullerton had a magnificent career and had rightly earned the reputation as one of Funny Cars finest drivers, this was his only national event victory.

All Uphill for Meyer

From racing karts to owning the Texas Motorplex, Billy Meyer had come a long way. In 1972, at the age of 16, Billy was the youngest person to earn a Funny Car

license behind the wheel of the Steakley Chevrolet–sponsored Camaro of Roger Grover. In 1972, at the age of 16, Billy became the youngest person to earn a Funny Car license. He accomplished the feat behind the wheel of Roger Grover's Steakley Chevrolet–sponsored Camaro. That fall, Meyer opened more than a few eyes when he won the Manufacturers Funny Car Championship at OCIR.

Meyer reached the final round by way of having one of the two quickest elapsed times of the first three rounds. Meyer recorded the low ET of the meet in round one when he defeated Jim Murphy with a 6.51 at 218 mph. In the final round, Meyer out-drove veteran Ron Olson, taking the win with a 7.37 to a fading 7.82. Meyer's victory combined with Richard Tharp's three-win outing in the *Blue Max* Mustang helped ensure Ford's winning of the meet. For Billy, his career was all uphill from there.

Pro Stock Mustangs or Hen's Teeth

In 1972, not many Mustangs competed in Pro Stock due to the unfavorable weight breaks. "Tiny" Tim McNalley was one of the few who gave it a shot. He did so with his 1970 Mustang.

Tim campaigned his Mustang through 1974, and although it was not the best fit for class, Tim managed to qualify the car at most of the shows he entered. Tim purchased his Mustang new in 1969 and ran the genuine Boss 429 car initially in Modified Production. He made the move to Pro Stock in 1971. In 1972, he updated the Mustang to appear as a 1970 model as NHRA rules stated that

In 1972, at the age of 16, Billy Meyer became the youngest person to earn a Funny Car license. That fall, he won the popular Manufacturers Funny Car Championship at OCIR. Seen here in 1973, Billy won his first of 18 national events, the IHRA Springnationals, in 1974 with the Mustang. Today, Billy owns the Texas Motorplex, the long-time home of the NHRA Fallnationals. In 1974, Billy debuted the sport's first Mustang II Funny Car. (Photo Courtesy Michael Pottie)

What Could Have Been

Dating back to the 1960s, the Funny Car had been dealing with several issues, including blower explosions and the ensuing fire that was sure to follow. More than one career was ended due to serious burns caused by burning fuel and oil. Another issue was trying to get the developed horsepower to the ground through tires that were completely inadequate. In 1971, several drivers looked at the evolution in dragsters to the rear-engine design and adopted the layout in hopes of eliminating a few of their own issues. Robert Contorelli was one of them.

Robert was a bucks-down racer who had previously campaigned a front-engine Top Fuel dragster. He graduated to Funny Car in 1971 and stretched his wallet to build this Mustang using the best parts available. He had SPE build him the chassis, which

The mid-engine Funny Car craze was in full swing when Robert Contorelli debuted this sleek Mustang. The car featured the best of parts but never reached its full potential. After its retirement from the drag strip, the Mustang became a part of the sand drag scene. (Steve Reyes Photography)

cradled a 417-ci Donovan aluminum Hemi. Covering the works was a much-modified Mustang shell sliced and diced by Ed Wills of *Mr. Ed* fame. The magnificent paint was laid by John Bolton.

The biggest problem Robert had was money. He seemingly spent all his coin in building the car and had little left to run it or develop it further. The Mustang ran a reported best of 6.89 before it was retired in 1972. The times were respectable for the day but a few tenths off the leaders.

cars had to be built within the last three years. In 1974, rules were changed extending this to five years.

Tim always ran the Mustang with a Boss 429 and counted on Sonny Bryant to prepare the motor. Initially,

the Mustang ran with a pro-shifted Toploader before Tim switched to a Lenco in 1973. That year, he also made the move to a four-link rear suspension. Although a full roll cage was added, the chassis remained an all-Ford product. The fastest legal time for the Mustang was a 9.47 at 148 mph, which was recorded before the car was retired in 1974.

Stocks and Super Stocks

The Stock category took on a whole new look in 1972 as the NHRA went to a pure stock format. That meant

This Southern California–based Boss 429-powered Mustang was campaigned by "Tiny" Tim McNally. In legal trim, it ran its best ETs in the 9.40s. As a Mountain-motor match racer, it reportedly ran ETs in the 8.50s. (Photo Courtesy Mark Hatchett)

In the 1960s, Ohio was well known for the fine Gassers that called the state home. In the 1970s, the story was similar with the number of quality Super Stock Mustangs. One of the many standouts was the West Union–based SS/H car of Barry McFarland that was driven by Jim Fisher. (Photo Courtesy Bob Martin)

minimal modifications, street tires, and closed exhaust. In addition, the category was now closed to any car older than 1963. Gone were the questionable Tri-Five Chevys, McKellar-cammed Pontiacs, and early Rocket Oldsmobiles—cars that for so long dominated the category.

Many established racers rejected the format change and vacated the category. Many of them ended up in Super Stock. In the face of dwindling numbers, the Mustang held its own, setting class records and grabbing wins at every major event. Returning to earn gold were Rusty Gillis, Ken McLellan, and Bob Glidden. Joining them were several names that we'd come to be familiar with, such as Frank Cottone, Jim Morgan, Tom Burnell, and John Blain. John drove Bob Glidden's 1968 Mustang to an SS/F class win at Indy (though Tom Burnell's name

was on the window), as Glidden himself took his convertible to SS/H honors.

Rise of the Mad Dog

When you mention the name Bob Glidden, many think of the years he dominated Pro Stock. Bob graduated to the Pro category in 1972 after running Stock and Super Stock for the previous 10 years.

His first Pro Stock race was the season-ending Supernationals, where it took a holeshot by Grumpy Jenkins to defeat Glidden and his Pinto in the final. For the Whiteland's Indianapolis resident, it was a long way from humble beginnings in 1962, when he purchased a 427 Galaxie from employer Ed Martin Ford in Indianapolis. Bob worked himself into the shop foreman position at

It's fairly easy to distinguish Bob Glidden's Super Stock Mustangs, whether it's one of the ragtops or a fastback. Prior to 1972, "Ed Martin" was spelled out in block letters; after 1971, "Ed Martin Ford" was in cursive. The cars were equally as potent. (Photo Courtesy Bob Martin)

The Gliddens' second convertible was campaigned through 1972 before Bob made the move into Pro Stock. The same year, Bob quit his job at Ed Martin Ford. (Photo Courtesy Bob Martin)

It was previously reported that by 1972, Bob Glidden was pulling in $3,000 a month racing his two Cobra Jet Mustangs. That year, he sold the two cars to help finance the purchase of his first Pro Stocker, the Gapp & Roush Pinto. (Photo Courtesy Bob Martin)

the dealership, which is where he met his future wife, Etta. Their first date saw Bob working on the Galaxie all afternoon and racing it that evening.

Bob raced Stock with an Ed Martin–sponsored 1965 Galaxie before moving into a Super Stock 1969 Cobra Jet Mustang. That year, he was convinced by fellow racer Gene Turnage to move south to Louisville, Kentucky, and come work for Bob Frensley Ford. Frensley had a good rapport with someone within Ford, and in 1969, he put together a drag team of his own. Gene drove a Super Stock Cobra Fairlane while initially Frensley drove a Super Stock CJ Mustang. Glidden took over the Mustang upon his arrival.

In 1970, they moved up to a pair of Holman-Moody-Stroppe–prepped Pro Stock Mavericks. Bob miraculously survived a crash in one of the cars when a front wheel came apart. When Ford pulled out of racing in 1970, Frensley backed off himself and dropped the support of the two cars. Bob moved back to Indiana where in 1971 he campaigned a red SS/HA 1969 Mustang convertible along with a 1968 fastback. Etta proved to be a pretty good driver herself and spent seat time in the convertible proving it.

Glidden won the Division 2 Super Stock title in 1970, which only enhanced his reputation for building winners. In 1971, he established Bob Glidden Race Cars and built engines for select customers into the mid-1970s.

Glidden sold the convertible to Lonnie Garner and obviously kicked himself for doing so as he built a nearly identical car in 1972. When Bob decided to make the jump to Pro Stock, he swung a deal with Gapp & Roush and purchased their Pinto. To help finance the deal he sold the fastback, the convertible, and the tow rig to Lonnie Garner. Lonnie turned around and sold the fastback to Clyde Brandon and partner Gene Turnage. Bob quit Ed Martin Ford at the end of 1972 and became a full-time drag racer, all the while growing the business.

Brandon & Turnage

As well as driving the Brandon & Turnage fastback, Gene spent some seat time in the convertible of Lonnie Garner in 1972. Gene started getting serious about drag racing behind the wheel of a 1956 Chevy. He switched to Ford when he went to work for Bob Frensley in 1969. Like so many, Frensley and Turnage first became acquainted at the track. Eventually, Turnage drove a big-block Chevelle that Bob owned. Turnage then drove a Mustang for the dealer before Glidden was lured south.

Brandon & Turnage had a lot of success with the ex-Glidden Mustang through early 1974, counting on a Glidden-built 428 to set records and win class. When building the bulletproof 428s Glidden followed the common practice of ensuring the bottom end was well oiled. According to Gene, they never had the bearing issues

As early as 1973, Gene Turnage ran the Mustang with either a 4-speed or C-6 to gain division points. Gene won the Division 2 points championship in 1975 on the strength of two national event wins, multiple class wins, and records set. (Photo Courtesy Bob Martin)

that many others did. Cold, the engine would read 100 psi of oil pressure.

"Bob was big on details," Gene said. "Nothing was left undone or left to chance. Internally the cylinders had a very slick finish, which cut the friction to nil. You could spin the snout of the crank freely with one hand. The engines ran fairly conventional bearing and ring gaps."

Running the Mustang with the so-called Canadian heads, the Mustang fell into SS/E where, in April 1973, Gene set the class ET record with a 10.83.

Behind the 428 rode a Doug Nash–prepped Toploader that carried a 2.78 first gear. To earn extra points, Brandon & Turnage swapped in a TCI-prepped C-6 with a three-grand convertor. When it came to the chassis and suspension, Gene stated that there was very little done to the car.

The Mustang was sold to Steve Retton of West Virginia in 1974 but not before the team picked up sponsorship from Toby Howard's Nitro 9, which was a company that produced fuel and oil additives. Toby called Clyde out of the blue one day and said, "I'd like to help you all."

The quick-witted Clyde responded with, "We'd like to have you help us."

The deal saw Toby provide the pair with a nice, plush motorhome to pull the car and a fair amount of financial support. It was a lucrative deal that lasted a few years before Nitro 9 disappeared.

Greater success came with the pair's second Mustang, another red 1968 fastback, which Gene refers to as the four-link car. A lot of work went into designing the

four-link suspension, as rules at the time didn't allow cutting of the floors. What made it work were rules that did allow a floating rear end. Gene set records in SS/E, SS/F, and SS/FA with the car, recording best of times in the 10.60s.

By late 1975, the men were doing their own engine work after opening their own shop outside of Nashville. They worked with Lunati and tested numerous "experimental" cams. These lasted about 10 runs, which was long enough to tell them what they needed to know.

Although the 428 was factored to 375 hp by the NHRA in 1975, the engines used by Brandon & Turnage were developing as much as 450 hp at 7,500 rpm on Glidden's dyno. New rules had the team running a Nash transmission behind the 428, which was backed by a 9-inch rear that housed a variety of gear sets ranging from 5.38 to 5.57 (depending on track conditions, tires, and whether the automatic transmission was being used). Tires had now grown to 14x32 in size.

In April 1975, Brandon & Turnage set their last record with the car in SS/E with a 10.57 at 128.75 mph. The Mustang was sold to Jeff Velde in the summer of 1975 but was campaigned by Clyde and Gene through the remainder of year. In 1976, Brandon & Turnage bought Glidden's old Pro Stock Pinto and campaigned it in C/Gas for the next three years before retiring.

1973: The More Things Change . . .

The year 1973 saw Mustang sales increase slightly to 134,867, up more than 10,000 from 1972. The car saw a

The Nitro 9-sponsored CJ Mustang of Brandon and Turnage was the car to beat in 1974-1975. The pair's first Mustang was sold to Steve Retton, who told them that if he knew they were going to build a second Mustang, he never would have bought the first one. (Photo Courtesy Bob Martin)

The 1971 through 1973 Mustang may not have shared the same popularity of early models, but it found a place on the track and did alright, whether it was a bracket bomber, Stocker, or Super Stocker. (Photo Courtesy Rob Potter)

minor face lift while the net horsepower of the top 351 came in at 259, a 16-hp drop over 1972 as the manufacturer moved to meet emission standards.

When it came to on-track pursuits, outside of Funny Car the 1973 Mustang had few takers. Those in Stock and Super Stock preferred the proven Cobra Jet Mustangs, and in Pro Stock, well, the weight breaks saw the Mustang on the outside looking in because the compacts were given breaks that made them unbeatable.

The Arne Swenson and Bob Lani Mustang from New Brunswick, New Jersey, usually qualified well and gave the big boys a run for the money. However, major victories eluded the team. S&W Race Cars built the chassis under this one, which held a 426-inch Hemi. (Photo Courtesy Michael Pottie)

Don Green opened eyes in the 1960s with his Rat Trap *AA/Fuel Altered Bantam before making the move to Funny Car in 1971. The* Rat Trap *Mustang debuted in 1973 and is driven here by Wayne Greiser. Although it was always a show stopper, major victory eluded the Mustang. (Photo Courtesy Michael Pottie)*

Tom Woodbridge and Jerry Baltes, business partners in Dragsters Inc. from Richmond, Virginia, campaigned this Mustang in 1973 with Harlan Thompson at the controls. Their best showing came at the IHRA Winternationals, where they made the semifinals before falling to Pat Foster. (Photo Courtesy Michael Pottie)

John Pusch and Don Cain were Top Gas standouts, winning the Division 5 title five times before the NHRA eliminated the class. In 1972, Pusch & Cain debuted this 392-powered Mustang and again won their division title. Captured here in 1973, Don retired after the 1974 season. (Photo Courtesy Michael Pottie)

The Colorado-based Hells Cargo Mustang of Ernie Spickler and Tom Cacy won its share of high-altitude races. The Mustang was an ex-Jerry Ruth Mustang that the team ran through 1976. (Photo Courtesy Tommy Shaw)

This beautiful Mustang belonged to the Southern California–based team of Plueger and Gyger. Through the early and mid-1970s, final-round appearances were a common occurrence for these guys, as they appeared at any number of California tracks to take home honors. (Photo Courtesy Michael Pottie)

Denny Fedele from Madison, Wisconsin, ran the Godfather *through 1973 in BB/FC. The former* Gold Digger *was later sold to future world champ Frank Hawley, who ran it as his first Funny Car. (Photo Courtesy Bob Martin)*

Funny Car

The Mustang remained a popular choice in both AA/FC and BB/FC through 1973. Although national event victories proved to be elusive during the bodystyle's final year, the Mustangs guaranteed to put on a worthy show thanks to several established racers and rising stars. Connie Kalitta was back wowing them with his Mustang. Don Green of *Rat Trap* Fuel Altered fame ran a Mustang Funny Car with Wayne Greiser behind the wheel. Keeling and Clayton, having mastered Top Fuel by winning the Supernationals in 1970 and joining the Cragar 5-Second Club in 1972, moved into a AA/FC Mustang in 1973. Jerry Baltes, whose career in Top Fuel dates back to the 1950s and included many national wins, partnered with Tom Woodbridge in running a Mustang. A few others worth mentioning are Colorado-based Ernie Speckler; Wisconsin's Denny Fedele, a former Top Gas standout; and the 1972 Division 5 champs Pusch and Cain.

Plueger & Gyger

Gerry Glenn, who drove the Steve Plueger, Ken Gyger AA/FC Mustang, was a seasoned driver with numerous Top Fuel wins under his belt, including the 1971 NHRA World Finals.

Driving for Plueger and Gyger in 1973, Glenn quickly proved his worth with a runner-up finish to Tom McEwen at one of the AHRA Grand-American races. At the AHRA World Finals, he repeated as runner-up when he fell to Jim Dunn in the final round. Plueger, who at the time was growing a reputation as a quality chassis builder, was himself a graduate of Top Fuel, having previously campaigned a car with Steve Carbone. A team effort in running a Fuel Altered followed before he hooked up with Gyger to run the Mustang. We heard from the team again in 1974, when Dave Condit drove the Mustang to a win at the 1974 World Finals, defeating the Dodge of Ed McCulloch in the final.

The Frantic Ford

The Frantic Ford team was another group who had previously established itself in the Top Fuel ranks before making the switch to Funny Car in 1969. In the 1960s, the team ran an AA/FD and was known as the Frantic Four. The team consisted of owner Jim Fox, Norm Weekly,

TOP RIGHT: *The Mustang of Mendes & Waters relied upon an engine built by Holman-Moody's Wally Cartwright to run record times. The team set the SS/GA record in September 1972 and held it for the next year. Mendes won SS/IA at the 1973 Winternationals with an 11.85 ET at 116.42 mph. (Photo Courtesy Dave Kommel)*

The second Frantic Ford Mustang was wheeled here by Rapid Roy Harris during the 1973 season. The Mustang was a terror throughout the East and Midwest. S&W built the chassis, and K&G Speed Associates helped with sponsorship. (Photo Courtesy Michael Pottie)

*The **Frantic Ford** Mustang II was driven by Dodger Glenn and tuned by Jim Fox. At the close of the 1977 season, the operation was sold to Glenn. Sadly, he died after an on-track incident in July 1978. (Photo Courtesy Michael Pottie)*

Ron Rivero, and top wrench Dennis Holding. Based in Southern California, the team's accolades included 1966 and 1967 NASCAR division championships and a win at Bakersfield in 1968.

In 1969, Fox moved to Broomall, Pennsylvania, and debuted the first in a line of four *Frantic Ford* Mustang Funny Cars. With Ron Rivero behind the wheel, the *Frantic Ford* became one of the East's most feared Funny Cars. The *Frantic Ford* went through several drivers, starting with Rivero. Sarge Arciero took over for 1971–1972, followed by Roy Harris in 1972–1973, and Dodger Glenn from 1974 to 1978.

Fox brought in Freddy Frey as part owner in the mid-1970s and hired on driver Dodger Glenn in 1974. Glenn bought out the operation in 1978 and carried on successfully under the Frantic Ford banner until his passing.

Stocks and Super Stocks

There were a total of 40 classes in Super Stock and another 48 in Stock. With fair ease, the early Mustangs held class records in a half dozen of those while winning their predicted classes at national events another dozen times.

Outside of Don Bowles, who continued to impress with his 1971 Mustang, there were few 1971–1973 models making waves at this point on the national level. Locally, the newer Mustang was gaining in popularity and as the decade progressed people learned to draw the most from the low-compression 351 engine.

Winners Galore

Kicking off the year and doing the Mustang proud were Winternationals class winners J. Mendes (SS/IA), John Turley (SS/F), Lonnie Garner (SS/N), and Brian Cour (SS/IA). Records seem to come just as easy as class wins.

Tom Burnell, a wrench man for Bob Glidden, built a 1969 Cobra Jet coupe and owned it just long enough to set the SS/H class record before selling it to Dan Crawley, who set the SS/G record with it before winning class at Indy with a 11.17 at 121.55 mph.

Harold Stout in the Stout & Crawley SS/H 1969 Mustang briefly held the class record with the former Glidden convertible and won his class at Indy with a 11.70 at 120.96 mph. Of course, Brandon & Turnage were back in Glidden's old Mustang to take the SS/F record in April with a 10.83 and SS/FA class at Indy

The Ulrey brothers (John, Jim, and Mike) had a lot of success in Stock and Super Stock. Although Jim had his success, John seemed to do the most winning. Along with the brothers' numerous wins through the early 1970s, John won the Division 3 Stock points championship in 1977. In 1976 and 1977, he won E/S at Indy. Mike won the I/S class trophy at Indy in 1970 and the C/SM class in a 1968 Mustang in 1976. (Photo Courtesy Bob Martin)

Harold Stout and Danny Crawley doubled down with their CJ coupe by running both SS/G and SS/GA. The car won the SS/G class at Indy in 1973, defeating Jeff Velde with an 11.17 ET at 121.55 mph. Bob Glidden gets credit for building the high-horsepower 428. (Photo Courtesy Bob Martin)

Harold Stout was the SS/H class winner at Indy in 1973, running an 11.20 ET at 120.96 mph to defeat the Camaro of Gary Hartsook. Danny Crawley purchased this car from Lonnie Garner, who purchased it from Glidden in 1972. (Photo Courtesy Bob Martin)

Cincinnati's Kenny Burton was a tough competitor in SS/O during 1973 with his 255-hp 289 1965 ragtop. (Photo Courtesy Bob Martin)

in the same car. All the while Turnage retained the SS/GA record.

Additional record setters included Jack Worrell, a graduate of 1960s Junior Stock (anyone remember his early 1950s Oldsmobile?), who hopped between his two King Cobra cars, his G/SA Fairlane, and his E/SA 1969 Mustang convertible.

Jack used the Fairlane to win class at Indy and his Mustang to set the top speed record at 106.50 mph. The irrepressible Steve Steele held the D/SA record with his 1969 Mustang with a 12.61 at 109.53 mph. Lonnie Garner held the SS/H record, relying upon Glidden power to get the job done.

Ken McLellan retained his SS/G record, and Brian Cour, the Oregon sports writer, used his 1968 Cobra Jet Mustang to grab the SS/HA record.

The early 289-powered Mustangs got in on the act when the Oregon team of Ferd and John Wardin set the SS/OA elapsed time record in their 1964 Mustang at 12.35.

The Super Stock Cobra Jet

Everyone had his or her own ideas on how to build a winning Cobra Jet Mustang, but there were basic consistencies that all the top performers followed. Good oiling and a strong bottom end were at the top of most people's list of necessity. By the mid-1970s, everyone had figured out that bearing life was limited by the fact that they were starved for oil. By blending the oil passages in the block to match the holes in the bearing shell, restricting the oil passages to the top end, and utilizing a high-volume oil pump, engine durability was greatly improved.

When it came to handling the torque of a good Super Stock Cobra Jet, the bottom end had to be beefed. Some ran the old-fashioned girdle early on, while others spared no expense and added 427-style cross-bolted four-bolt mains. Still others felt secure in sticking with the factory two-bolt main caps. The NHRA initially banned the use of the cross-bolted mains.

In 1968, Dave Lyall tried to run a 406 block (some were side-bolted stock and carried the same bore as a 428) and got busted. Others used the side bolts and did their best to hide them by counter-sinking the bolts and filling the holes.

By 1971, the NHRA had become a little lax on the rule, as a few racers ran them openly. Tony Rainero for one was

running them in his SS/H Mustang. To further strengthen the block, some racers filled the water jackets to the frost plugs with an oven cement.

Like the Cleveland, the 428 suffered from thin cylinders. It was recommended by most builders that the cylinders not to be opened more than 0.020 to 0.030 over the stock bore. Any more than that, and you'd quickly encounter bore distortion, poor seal, and possibly cracked cylinders. To get around the issue, several racers hogged-out the cylinders and went to thicker sleeves. This not only eliminated the inherited problem but it also allowed them to take advantage of the NHRA 0.065-over rule. By the end of the decade, that rule had increased to 0.080 over, resulting in 443 ci (almost the same as putting a 428 crank in a 427 block minus 10 cubic inches).

Through the 1970s, NHRA rules limited one's choice of which pistons and rods could be used. In 1978, Venolia released Super Stock-legal gas-ported pistons to fill those enlarged cylinders. When it came to camshafts, ignition, and intake manifolds, the rules pretty much left the door open. Porting and polishing was a no-no, but it didn't stop some from modifying the ports and hiding "acid porting." What's the old saying? It's only cheating if you get caught.

CHAPTER 5

1974-1978
IT'S A MUSTANG TOO

TOP: *When Chrysler dropped support of Herb McCandless in 1973, he began racing Fords–first with a Pinto Pro Stocker and then behind the wheel of this Lou Oleynik-owned 1974 Mustang II. The Don Hardy-chassis car was last raced by McCandless at the 1975 IHRA Spring Nationals before being sold to Bob Glidden. (Photo Courtesy Mike Dimery)*

Although true enthusiasts had an issue with Ford sticking the Mustang name on what was perceived to be little more than an overblown Pinto, the general public liked the redesign enough that it bought 386,000 units the first year. The Mustang II, as it was pegged, saw little change throughout its five-year cycle. The standard engine was a 4-cylinder with the only option the first year being a V-6. A 302 became available 1975, but with a net horsepower rating of 122, it was shunned like the plague by those looking to race.

1974: Pony Time

You could say that 1974 was the year in which Pro Stock truly became a professional category. Full-tube chassis were permitted, and cars that just a year before were being built using bodies in white were now pieced

Rich Simone debuted his Mustang II in 1974 after campaigning a Pro Stock Maverick. Rich ran the Mustang through 1980 and produced ETs in the 8.70s. (Photo Courtesy Michael Pottie)

The Trojan Horse Mustang of Kevin Doheny and Larry Fullerton debuted in 1974. Although it was always a popular draw, major event victory eluded the Mustang. AMT made a popular 1/25-scale kit of the Mustang II. (Photo Courtesy Michael Pottie)

together with individual panels. The Mustang II's compact outer dimensions and favorable aerodynamics made it an immediate success in the category. The same reasons made the car a Funny Car favorite.

Funny Car

All the news that was fit to be news in Funny Car happened at the NHRA World Finals. The race found a new home in 1974, as the NHRA moved the race from Amarillo, Texas, to the spacious Ontario Motor Speed-

In 1975, Bill Leavitt reappeared with a Mustang II. At the NHRA Winternationals he held the number-1 qualifying position with an ET of 6.21 and reached the semifinals before bowing out. Although an NHRA national event victory eluded Bill, he had success early on in AHRA and IHRA competition. (Photo Courtesy Michael Pottie)

way. This was the first year in which world championships were decided by points instead of the previous format, where points were used only to determine who could compete at the event. The old way had the race winner being crowned the world champ.

The World Finals

The biggest story of the year came at the World Finals. No, it wasn't the final-round win by Dave Condit, but I'll start there. Dave, driving the Pluger & Gyger 1972 Mustang, pulled off what many deemed to be an upset in the final round when he defeated Ed McCullogh's Revell-sponsored Duster with a hair-raising 6.24 to a losing 6.33. Through the lights, the Donovan Hemi in Condit's ride saw a couple of rods ventilate the block. The spewing oil ignited on the hot headers creating a fireball from which Dave was lucky to escape.

"David got the car stopped so fast, the chutes blew past him," Crewman Tommy Naccarato said. "He was so excited after he got out of the car, jumping around, that the safety safari thought he was on fire and started squirting him off!"

Chained Lightning

As exciting as the final round was, the real story of the event was Shirl Greer's return after a blower explosion during qualifying had sent him to the hospital and all but destroyed the body of his 1972 Mustang.

Shirl had been having a great year, winning rounds, and earning a class win at the Grandnationals in Canada by defeating the Chevy Vega of Kosty Ivanof. Coming

There's nothing scarier than a top-end Funny Car fire, and Shirl Greer's fireball at the 1974 World Finals was one of the worst. He returned the next day, with a lot of help from friends. (Photo Courtesy Howard Koby/Lou Hart Archives)

After rushed repairs, Greer and the Mustang came back to win the first round of eliminations against the Chadderton and Okazaki Vega, which was enough to lock in the world title. (Photo Courtesy Michael Pottie)

into the World Finals, Shirl was trailing Paul Smith in the standings by 174 points. Greer got a break when Smith failed to qualify. Hot on Greer's heals was Don Prudhomme, who also had a shot at the title. It was going to take Greer more than a little luck to pull off a championship win.

Any hopes Shirl had of winning appeared to have been snuffed during qualifying when a massive top-end fire sent him to the hospital with second-degree burns to his hands and face. The Mustang barely survived with extensive fire damage done to the back half of the car. In a show of the obvious comradery that engulfs the sport of drag racing, a few dozen of Greer's peers jumped in and proceeded to piece the Mustang back together again in anticipation of Greer's return. The rear body was rebuilt using sheet aluminum, a boatload of rivets, and yards to "racer's tape." Tom Hanna, Paul Smith, Don

Prudhomme, and crew all contributed time and parts.

Against doctors' wishes, Shirl signed himself out of the hospital the next day with full intentions of getting back behind the wheel of the now-repaired car. Donning a pair of gloves, provided by Prudhomme, Greer took his one shot at qualifying and made it.

In eliminations, Greer defeated Leroy Chadderton in the Chadderton and Okazaki Chevy Vega in the first round. This gave him the points needed to clinch the title as Prudhomme lost in the second round to Dale Pulde.

Greer and his *Chained Lightning* Mustang, and the Mustang II that followed in 1976, went on to win numerous AHRA, IHRA, and NHRA national events, but nothing as dramatic as the World Finals win in 1974.

Mustangs Return to Pro Stock

The 96-inch-wheelbase Mustang II proved to be a good fit in Pro Stock where the ever-changing weight breaks favored the short-wheelbase car when powered by a reworked Cleveland or Boss 302. Racers who debuted Mustang IIs in 1974 were Stacey Shields Jr., Herb McCandless, Don Nicholson, and the team of Wayne Gapp and Jack Roush. Previously each of them had campaigned a Pro Stock Pinto.

Both Dyno Don and the 1973 World Championship–winning team of Gapp & Roush debuted Don Hardy–built Mustangs at the NHRA Gatornationals. Gapp qualified the Mustang II number-2 at the race, laying down a 9.03

Don Nicholson's new Mustang II made a good showing during its debut at the NHRA Gatornationals in 1974 but fell in eliminations to eventual category winner Wally Booth. The "$ Patty $" on the C-pillar was a nod to Don's wife. She handled the finances, helped with bookings, and traveled regularly with Don. (Photo Courtesy Michael Pottie)

against Booth. Booth repeated his previous 8.97 to defeat Gapp's 9.01.

Gapp & Roush

Gapp & Roush accomplished quite a bit over the eight years the team was together. While Wayne Gapp was campaigning his injected Funny Car in 1969, Jack Roush was teamed with the Fastbacks, a group of Ford engineers that first appeared in 1965. Jack left Ford in the later 1960s and briefly went to work for Chrysler before taking a job as a teacher at a junior college. Wayne hired him from there to run the day-to-day operations of his Performance Engineering.

The pair's first team car was a Boss 429–powered Pro Stock Maverick. A variety of Fords followed (Pintos, Mavericks, and the Mustang II), as did a long list of national event wins. During the period the men developed a reputation as they built engines of various sizes for several teams in pretty much every category. Their specialty? The Cleveland, of course. As well as engines, they produced and sold several parts under the Gapp &

at 152.88 mph. Nicholson qualified down in the pack with a 9.12. He improved to a 9.03 in the first round of eliminations, but it wasn't enough to defeat Wally Booth, whose AMC Hornet recorded an 8.97. Gapp went on to set low ET of the meet and top speed running an 8.88 and 153.06 while on route to a final-round appearance

In 1974, the release of the Mustang II spelled the end of the Pinto in Pro Stock. The team of Gapp & Roush saw some success with its Mustang II before rule changes saw the team make the switch to a longer-wheelbase four-door Maverick. (Photo Courtesy Michael Pottie)

Few built horsepower like the team of Gapp & Roush. The Cleveland propelled the Mustang II to a runner-up finish at the Gatornationals, turning low ET and top speed of the meet with an 8.94 at 153.06 mph. (Photo Courtesy Todd Wingerter)

The Harvey Cohen Quick Trip *Mustang was one of three 1970 models that Don Hardy built. John Healey drove this one in 1974 and 1975 before it was sold to the team of Talitsch & Buono in 1976. (Photo Courtesy Dan Williams)*

Roush name: high-port Boss 429 heads, raised-exhaust plates for the 351, intake manifolds, conversion kits for stuffing a small-block V-8 into a Pinto, the list goes on. In 1978, the pair went its separate ways, and as history has shown, on to bigger and better things.

The Breaks

The only constant in NHRA Pro Stock during the 1970s, outside of Ford wins, was change. Weight breaks were constantly being adjusted in an attempt to halt the Cleveland-powered Fords. Revised breaks midseason ended up favoring longer-wheelbase cars because cars with a wheelbase over 105 inches had to carry 6.45 lbs/ci, whereas cars under a 105-inch wheelbase had to carry 6.85 lbs/ci. You can see how the Mustang II fell out of favor with some.

Four racers chose to build longer-wheelbase 1970 model Mustangs to take advantage of the new breaks: Don Nicholson, Harvey Cohen, and Bob Glidden each

While Dyno continued to march on with his Mustang II in AHRA and IHRA competition (and winning numerous national events), he debuted a longer wheelbase, NHRA-suited 1970 Mustang here at the NHRA Grandnationals in 1974. His first pass with the car netted an ET of 9.07. (Photo Courtesy Bob Boudreau)

debuted Don Hardy–chassis cars, while the team of Davis & Sain later debuted what is believed to have been a Joe Smith–chassis car. Oddly, the team of Gapp & Roush chose to go with an unconventional long-wheelbase four-door Maverick.

The Pro Stock Cleveland

How would you build a competitive Cleveland in the mid-1970s? Obviously, you would start with a four-bolt main block, either by drilling out an existing quality

If you wonder what made Bob Glidden a dominant force in 1970s Pro Stock, you're looking at it: the heavily modified Edelbrock intake sports twin Holley Dominator carburetors atop the Cleveland. Camshaft specifications by the later part of the decade was in the neighborhood of 0.800 lift, 330 duration.

Exhaust-port plates increased power by raising the ports, removing the factory "dog leg." Improvements over factory ports were large on a high-horsepower, higher-RPM Pro Stock engine. These square units are found on one of Bob Glidden's Clevelands.

block or by using a Boss 302 or 1971 Cleveland block. From there, it was standard fare to go with an internally balanced crank. Although the factory externally balance crank worked fine in a stocker, it whipped in a high-RPM Pro Stock engine and took out bearings and ruined parts.

To help further increase bearing life, oil was rerouted from the top end. The problem with the Cleveland lies in the fact that the main gallery runs front to rear through the right side of the block and opens up to each lifter bore. Pull the lifters on a Cleveland, and you can see large egg-shaped oil holes that intersect with the main galley. These holes are too large and flood the top end with oil, starving the bottom end. A high-pressure oil pump was used, but by 1974 the dry-sump system was coming into vogue. This not only helped the oiling but the shallow pan also allowed racers to get the nose of the car down on the ground and out of the air.

Bore and stroke saw engines ranging in size from 331 up to 377 ci. At the time, Brooks Racing Pistons was the go-to for rods and pistons. Compression varied but ratio in the 12.5:1 to 13:1 range seemed standard. Dykes top ring and gas porting helped ensure a good seal. It's been reported that Bob Glidden couldn't live with anything greater than 3-percent leakage. Anything beyond that dictated a teardown and freshen up.

It was the Cleveland's large canted valves that really made the engine come alive. It was agreed by everyone that the shape of the exhaust ports on the 4V heads was wrong. The "dog leg" design created a dead spot that hampered flow. This was rectified by slicing the heads and adding an exhaust-port plate. Both Buddy Moore and Gapp & Roush had these plates available as early as 1972. What the plates did was raise the port approximately 1.5 inches and eliminated the dead spot.

Additional reworking of the ports and chambers was either done in-house, if you had the equipment, or by trusted guys such as C. J. Batten or Bob Mullen. As far as the intake manifolds go, a modified Edelbrock UR-19 tunnel ram with twin Holley dominators was the proven choice. Of course, any modifications to the carburetors or intake (plenum size and runners) were a well-kept secret by most.

Camshaft specs fell under the same category, but lift hovered around 0.725 in 1974. Estimated horsepower for a top-running engine was pegged right around 700 and produced 8.80 times.

Stocks and Super Stocks

Unlike the fluctuating weight breaks in the Pro Stock category, there were no rule changes in Stock or Super Stock that affected the Mustang's ongoing success. The

Division 3 standout Jim McClay and his SS/HA coupe are caught in action here at the 1974 U.S. Nationals. Although the Mustang was capable of 11.40 times, Jim failed to make it through class eliminations. (Photo Courtesy Bob Martin)

The Border Bandits lived on in Dave Freeman's 1969 ragtop. Dave had purchased John Elliott's 1968 CJ fastback, but when it was wrecked in a highway incident, he swapped the good parts that remained onto this car. John Blain is driving the car here at the Grandnationals in 1974. (Photo Courtesy Bob Boudreau)

aging CJ Mustangs refused to give quarter and continued to shine in Stock and Super Stock. Class wins continued to roll in from the usual suspects of Gene Turnage, Steven Steele, and Carl Holbrook. One name you could add to the list in 1974 was that of Frank Cottone.

Frank Cottone: Who, You Say?

To the less informed, Frank Cottone seemed to come out of nowhere with his SS/GA 1969 Mustang to win class at the Gatornationals, Springnationals, Summernationals, and Indy. He closed the season as runner-up at the World Finals, falling inches short to the Chevy of Bobby Warren.

Frank, a body man by trade, bought the Q-code (non-Ram Air) Mustang new in 1969 after having his fun with a 271-hp 1966 fastback. His intention from the get-go was to go racing with the Mustang so when he ordered the car, the only options checked off were the driveline and tinted glass. Frank initially ran the Mustang as a Stocker, taking F/SA class at the 1971 Summernationals. When the NHRA changed the rules of Stock at the end of the 1971 season Frank made the move to Super Stock. As well as the four class wins in 1974, Frank set and reset the SS/GA class

To say 1974 was a good year for Frank Cottone would be an understatement. Class wins seemed to come with ease. Frank bought his Mustang new and still owns it, having restored the car to Day 2 status. (Photo Courtesy Robert Kornegay)

Frank Cottone's SS/GA CJ Mustang was a powerhouse. Frank worked as a body man and painted the Mustang nearly every year. Silver being the go-to color. Backing the C-6 was usually 5.14 gears. (Photo Courtesy Tommy Cooksey)

record with the Mustang four times between 1972 and 1975.

Frank found no real weak link in the driveline. As a means of strengthening the block he filled the water jackets with hardening cement, material he received from NASCAR legend Richard Petty. Not a bad idea as many racers were doing it. Frank was one of the first to use the material. In hindsight, Frank figures he should have only filled the bottom half of the jackets as he had problems with the engine overheating. You live and learn. Any oiling concerns relating to the bottom end were dealt with by drilling out passages.

Frank retired the Mustang at the end of 1977 and built himself a Super Stock Cougar. Although he ran that car for the next 10 years before retiring, he never saw the same success as he had with the Mustang.

So-Cal's Finest

I've talked about several dealer-sponsored and club cars (Paul Harvey, Stark Hickey, and Foulger), but few could compare to the sheer number of competitive cars that carried the name of Southern California's Wilson Ford.

Although he was not directly dealer sponsored, Wilson Drag Club Member Marcel Cloutier won Super Stock at the 1974 NHRA Winternationals with his SS/FA 1968 Mustang. Marcel defeated Lloyd Bray's 1968 Mustang for class with an 11.47 at 119.84 mph before marching on to the finals where he faced and defeated the SS/CA Road Runner of Dave Wren with a record-setting 11.30. By the end of the season, Cloutier had dropped the class record to an 11.07 at 122.62 mph.

Wilson Drag Club Member Norm Nevin was responsible for building the Cobra Jet engine in Cloutier's car, as well as the engine in the SS/HA 1970 Mustang Wilson campaigned with driver Norm Nevin. What was difference between the two Mustangs (besides the years)? Cloutier's was a Ram Air car that carried flat-top pistons with 11.5:1

compression and an NHRA 360-hp rating. The Stafford & Nevin Mustang, driven by Nevin was factored to 340 hp and ran dished pistons and 11:1 compression. Beyond that, both engines were pretty much the same.

Ensuring a good foundation, Nevin had the blocks fitted with cross-bolted main caps. When it came to the

Marcel Cloutier's SS/FA Mustang won Super Stock Eliminator at the 1974 NHRA Winternationals. Marcel was one of the original Wilson Ford Drag Club members, along with Steve Steele and Tom Stafford (engine builder for Cloutier and others). (Photo Courtesy Dave Kommel)

Norm Nevin shows the pan and windage tray for his and Tom Stafford's Cobra Jet Mustang. Special baffling within the pan was designed by Norm. Oil fed through a 427 pump. Note the cross-bolted main caps and machined spacers.

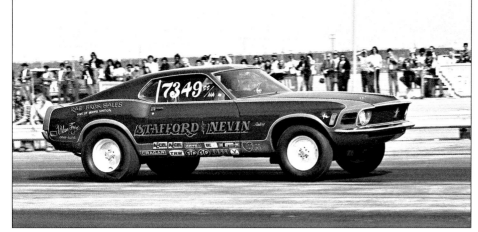

With Tom Stafford at the controls and Norm Nevin building the Cobra Jet, this 1970 Cobra Jet Mustang was an SS/HA winner. Tom is caught in action here at Bakersfield in 1974. (Photo Courtesy Dave Kommel)

choice of camshafts, both Clay Smith and Sig Erson shafts were swapped in and out. Both cams were said to run 0.640 lift. Filling the cylinders were Brook pistons. Up top, several intakes were tried, including a Sidewinder. As in the case of all medium-riser intake manifolds going onto a Cobra Jet, material needed to be added to the bottom of the ports to properly match the heads.

As the NHRA allowed the use of aftermarket carbs in Super Stock, as long as they had the same flow rate as the factory carb, the factory 735 Autolite carbs were replaced with Holley units. As described in a long-ago *Car Craft* magazine article, modifications to the Holleys was kept to a minimum: fuel-jet extenders were added on the secondaries, the secondary diaphragm spring saw one coil cut off, and the check ball was replaced by a slightly smaller one. A Phillips screwdriver was used to dimple the check-ball seat, which sped up the vacuum actuation of the secondaries. To light the air-fuel mixture a Hays ignition sent spark to Autolite plugs.

1975: Weathering the Storm

When it came to the 1975 Mustang, little had changed in performance or styling. Although the Mustang still led all pony cars in sales, sales were down from nearly 200,000 units to 188,575 units. Performance had become a bad word across the board, and the pony car was hit hard. Plymouth no longer offered the Barracuda, and Chevy dropped the Z/28.

When it came to on-track results, well, that was a whole different story.

ETs took a noticeable drop in Stock and Super Stock due to several rule changes, including how slicks up to 12 inches in width were now allowed in Stock, while in Super Stock, tires up to 15x33 in size were now accepted. Further changes in Super Stock allowed rear frame rails

"Rapid" Roy Harris was a popular Division 1 racer who hailed from Drexell Hill, Pennsylvania. From 1975 through 1978, he ran Mustangs under the Brutus label after purchasing the name from Lew Arrington. Harris had previously driven for the Frantic Ford team as well as "Jungle" Jim Liberman. (Photo Courtesy Michael Pottie)

A heavy hitter out of the Northwest was John Smith from Port Orchard, Washington. The Olympic Auto-sponsored Mustang was also driven on occasion by fellow Washington resident Jeff Wittig. The Mustang was an SS/F record holder in 1975.

to be moved inboard "moderately" to accommodate tire clearance. Also, it was now acceptable for unibody cars to tie the chassis front to back.

The NHRA introduced the index system (the no-breakout way of racing) to the Sportsman categories in 1975. Cars could now run flat out without taking the chance of breaking out, running too fast, and losing. Each index was determined by plugging information into a computer, such as the average runs of each class from all the national events in 1974.

Funny Car

As far as pure entertainment value, few classes of cars gave you more bang for your buck than the Funny Car. Only Pro Stock and Top Fuel came close. Funny Car fell between the two. Fans enjoyed the 1/8-mile burnouts, quarter-mile times that rivalled some Top Fuel cars, and bodies with which they could identify. Sure, pretty much all of them now ran Chrysler Hemis or aftermarket derivatives, but they still had the appearance of a production car, although less and less with each passing year.

The California Charger *Mustang of John Keeling and Jerry Clayton saw success through 1976. A number of drivers piloted the Mustang, including veteran Jake Johnston, seen here in 1974. Keeling & Clayton had gained national prominence in 1970 when the team won Top Fuel at the 1970 Supernationals. (Photo Courtesy Lou Hart)*

With Raymond Beadle at the helm, the Blue Max *proved to be one of the 1970s most dominant Funny Cars. Between 1975 and 1981, Raymond won three NHRA world titles and three IHRA world titles. (Photo Courtesy Dan Williams)*

The Blue Max *Reins*

Talking about bang for your buck, few Funny Cars were as rewarding to watch as Harry Schmidt's line of *Blue Max* Mustangs. Driver Raymond Beadle more than earned his keep in 1975 by winning the IHRA World Championship. Raymond accomplished the feat on the back of wins at the Winternationals, Pro-Am Nationals (where Shirl Greer was runner-up), Summernationals, and Nationals. After playing runner-up to Don Prudhomme at the NHRA Springnationals, Beadle defeated the Snake at the U.S. Nationals and set the class record along the way with a 6.14.

The *Blue Max* Funny Car has been around since 1970, when Schmidt debuted the first Mustang at the NHRA Winternationals. The line of Mustangs became one of the most prominent funnies of the 1970s. Jake Johnston, who gained a reputation driving and wrenching for Gene Snow, was the first to drive the *Blue Max* when the car debuted at the NHRA Winternationals. There, Johnston set top speed of the meet with a 203.61. Powering the Mustang was a Ramchargers-built Hemi that rode on a Don Hardy chassis.

At OCIR's annual manufacturers meet in November 1970, Jake recorded a 6.72 at 217.91, which was the quickest ET for a Funny Car up to that point. Shortly after, Johnston returned to the Snow camp. Richard Tharp next took the seat and drove for Schmidt through mid-1973, winning several IHRA events and a countless number of match races during his tenure. By late 1973, Schmidt was feeling burnt out and decided to take a brief hiatus from racing. In late 1974, he returned with a Tony

Harry Schmidt's Blue Max *Mustang made its debut at the NHRA Winternationals in 1970 where it set top speed of the meet with a 203.61 mph. Jake Johnston, a former wrench for Gene Snow, found happiness behind the wheel of the Don Hardy car, which was powered by a Ramchargers-built Hemi. (Photo Courtesy Don Prieto)*

Casarez–chassied *Blue Max* Mustang II with Raymond Beadle now at the controls.

Shortly after the team defeated Prudhomme at the 1975 U.S. Nationals, Schmidt sold the operation to Beadle. It wouldn't be an overstatement to say things took off from there with IHRA World titles coming in both 1975 and 1976. More world titles would follow. Although, midway through 1978, the Mustang shell gave way to a Plymouth Arrow.

Raymond Beadle made the move from Top Fuel to Funny Car in 1973 when he took the wheel of Don Schumacher's Vega. Late in 1974, he signed up with Harry Schmidt to drive the Blue Max. *Success immediately followed. (Photo Courtesy Michael Pottie)*

Pro Stock

There were nine class weight breaks to start the NHRA season with short-wheelbase Cleveland-powered Fords (Pintos and Mustang IIs) carrying the same weight as Chrysler's Hemi cars (7.30 lbs/ci). At the end

Eddie Schartman's Boss 429 Mustang II was his last ride after a long and lustrous career. The car was built as a match racer after Ed walked away from running Pro Stock. Capable of low-8 ETs, Ed ran the Mustang until he retired from the sport in 1975. (Photo Courtesy Bill Truby)

The NHRA added 0.35 lbs/ci to the long-wheelbase Clevelands in mid-1975, killing the advantage that guys such as Nicholson, Glidden, and Gapp & Roush had enjoyed running the long-wheelbase cars. (Photo Courtesy Todd Wingerter)

Bob and Etta made a great team. In the 1970s, Etta was recognized as one of Pro Stocks top crew chiefs. Grumpy Jenkins paid the Gliddens the ultimate compliment years later when he said that the Gliddens deserved everything they received and that no one worked harder. (Photo Courtesy Dave Wible)

of the season, the Mustang had seven national event wins (AHRA, IHRA, and NHRA) to Chrysler's one.

Glidden Pours It On

Bob Glidden, the 1974 NHRA Pro Stock World Champ, gave the 1970 Mustang its only national event wins when he opened the season by winning the AHRA and NHRA Winternationals and the NHRA Gatornationals. He defeated Wally Booth at the AHRA race and the Maverick of Gapp & Roush at both NHRA races. Both Glidden and Gapp & Roush switched back to their previous Pintos for the IHRA Winternationals, this time with Gapp coming out on top.

Glidden ran four different cars through 1975 and still managed to win seven national events and the world title. He debuted a Don Ness Mustang II in April and crashed it not long after at National Trails. He raced the 1970 Mustang through to the Summernationals at which point he sold the car and purchased the Don Hardy Mustang II of Lou Oleynik that had been driven by Herb McCandless. Glidden borrowed his 1974 World Champ Pinto back from the team of Clyde Brandon & Gene Turnage after falling early at the U.S. Nationals to the 1970 Mustang of Don Nicholson. Glidden closed the season with the Pinto, winning the Fallnationals and World Finals.

Bob and Etta are caught thrashing between rounds at the 1975 NHRA Summernationals to replace the broken Cleveland in their 1970 Mustang. Note the rod-produced hole in the oil pan. (Photo Courtesy Dave Wible)

As well as winning seven national events in 1975, Bob Glidden qualified number-1 at five national events, ran low ET six times, and held top speed eight times. Here at the 1975 IHRA Summernationals, Bob and his Don Ness Mustang II are guided from the water box by Etta Glidden. (Photo Courtesy Dan Williams)

Bob Glidden ran the ex-Hauler Mustang at four events in 1975: the Tri-City WCS race, which he won; the NHRA Grandnationals; and the PHR Championship races, both of which he lost to Maskin & Kanners in the second round. His last race of the year was at the NHRA U.S. Nationals, where he lost in the third round to the 1970 Mustang of Don Nicholson. (Photo Courtesy Rob Potter)

In the 1975 *National Dragster* Pro Stock championship issue, Glidden said that the Ness car was going to race IHRA races. Because he had two cars at the time (a 1970 Mustang for NHRA and the Mustang II), the engine program suffered a series of engine failures. Glidden blamed this on the toll it took to run the two-car operation. The setback saw Gapp & Roush briefly take the lead in the NHRA points standings. Glidden reacted by restructuring his operations. He sold both cars, reclaimed the Pinto, and once again won the points championship and world title.

Like many Ford Pro Stock racers, Glidden ran Clevelands of various sizes. Continuously, the Cleveland combinations were being hit by the NHRA with more weight, which only made the Glidden team work harder to find power. Many hours were spent reworking cylinder heads: reshaping chambers, reshaping ports, raising ports, and adjusting the size of the ports. Almost as much work went into the intake manifold, where plenums were reshaped and shrunk and runners were reshaped to straighten the flow. It's no wonder that even through all the turmoil of the year the Gliddens still held the class record through most of the season, recording a best of 8.72 at 156.25 mph in December.

Dyno(mite) Don

Although NHRA national event wins eluded Dyno Don through 1975, he continued his winning ways in match racing and did more than alright for himself in IHRA competition, where he won the World

Championship.

In July, Don defeated Scott Shafiroff at the Summernationals held at Union Grove. Dyno used a slight holeshot to beat Scott's Mustang II, turning in a 9.01 at 149.00 mph to Shafiroff's 8.98 at 150.50. At Dragway 42 in August, Don continued on his march to the championship by defeating Roy Hill in the ex–Butch Leal Duster. Don defeated the Duster of low-qualifier Don Carlton in the second round when Carlton backed off after get-

Dyno Don ran this Mustang II at all AHRA and IHRA races he attended through 1975. The car is seen here at Great Lakes for the IHRA Summernationals, a race that Don won. Note the pulled-in bumpers and drooped nose to help cheat the wind. (Photo Courtesy Dan Williams)

The Edelbrock dyno at El Segundo, California, was put to use by many racers. Here (in this late-1973 photo) is one of Dyno Don's Clevelands ready for a pull.

ting out of shape. In the semifinals, Hill defeated Larry Huff while Dyno put away "General" Lee Edwards. In the final go, Hill's 9.04 at 153.84 mph wasn't quite enough to beat Don's 9-flat at 154.84.

In Pro Stock, it was standard fare to run sleeved Cleveland blocks because the factory cylinders generally lost their shape and failed after a handful of runs. Nicholson discovered just how bad the factory castings were when machinist Bill Coon

Stacy Shields Jr. and partner Willie Warlow were always top contenders, whether in Super Stock or Pro Stock. Their Norm Paddock Mustang II was powered by a Gapp & Roush mill and tuned with the help of crewman John Humphrey. The Indianapolis-based Mustang realized 9.0 ETs at 150 mph in 1975. (Photo Courtesy Steve Reyes)

Chassis builder Norm Paddack tried his hand at Pro Stock after a successful run behind the wheel of a few Opel Gassers and a Vega Funny Car. He debuted this Mustang II in 1975. Renowned Michigan engine builder Sam Gianino took care of the Cleveland, which propelled the car well into the 9s. Norm is caught here on the return road of the National Trail during the 1975 Springnationals. (Photo Courtesy Todd Wingerter)

A Chevy guy through and through, Scott Shafiroff tried his hand running a Mustang II in 1975. He was rewarded with a win at the IHRA Springnationals in Bristol. (Photo Courtesy Michael Pottie)

This was a state-of-art-the Pro Stock car in 1975. There is no doubt that Scott Shafiroff had a learning curve going from Chevy to Ford. The chassis was by Don Hardy. (Photo Courtesy Dave Wible)

Steve Deniston was SS/G class winner in 1977 at Indy recording an ET of 10.82 at 124.82 mph. A Carl Holbrook–built CJ got the job done. (Photo Courtesy Dave Kommel)

ran a hone through one of his Clevelands and revealed numerous high spots. The hone would jump all over the place. It was Don who presented the idea of sleeving the blocks to Coon, who then sourced chrome-moly sleeves in California.

Replacing the factory cylinders with 0.275-inch-thick barrels was a pretty straightforward process for Coon, who was a well-qualified machinist and had the equipment and resources to get it done. After the factory cylinders were cut out, blocks were cleaned and copper plated. This ensured a good bond when the works was furnace brazed together. After the brazing, the block was then line honed, decked, and bored. The thick sleeves made the possibilities nearly endless. For example, both Dyno and Glidden made use of a 4.140-inch bore and a 3.50-inch stroke combination that yielded 377 ci.

Stocks and Super Stocks

The NHRA continuously played the horsepower-factor game, nailing any combination that showed an advantage over another. The 1975 factors for the 428 were as follows: a CJ with flat-top pistons was rated at 370 hp, a dished piston CJ was rated at 360 hp, and a Canadian-head flat-top piston CJ was rated a 380 hp. With the number of competent Stock and Super Stock engine builders squeezing the most out of the CJ, you'd be hard pressed to pick a gentleman who stood out above the rest.

Captain Cobra Jet

In 1975, Carl Holbrook, also known as Captain Cobra Jet, was at the top of his game. Carl started out his racing career running dirt tracks in the early 1960s. He bought his first Mustang, a 1967 that was powered by a Tony Rainero–built 390. Eyes were drawn to Carl in 1969 when he purchased a CJ Mustang and started to compile wins. Several Mustangs followed, as did a string of class wins and records. His stats were all that more impressive considering the fact that he rarely traveled outside of his Division 3 area.

After spending a few years building engines out of his home garage for himself and a select few, increased demand forced him to open his own shop in 1973. By that time, the Captain Cobra Jet moniker had taken hold.

Stacey Shields enjoyed much success with his SS/FA Mustang. As early as 1970, the Mustang held class record and was winning divisional races. The Mustang is seen here at the 1975 NHRA Springnationals, where Stacey also showed up with his Pro Stock Mustang II. Leonard Richards drove the Super Fly II, *which had a Carl Holbrook 428 under the hood. (Photo Courtesy Todd Wingerter)*

Carl Holbrook set his first class record in this Mustang at Saginaw, Michigan, in July 1971. Running SS/GA, the Mustang recorded an 11.45 ET. The record stood through August 1972. (Photo Courtesy Michael Mihalko)

From Livonia, Michigan, Carl Holbrook ran this SS/GA Mustang convertible in 1975. The Instant Action Mustang was a class winner and record holder with an 11.07 ET, and it was capable of 10.80 times. (Photo Courtesy Bob Martin)

Carl Holbrook's 1969 Mustang had many class wins under its belt, helping to establish Carl's "Captain Cobra Jet" title. By 1973, Carl began building engines for other racers. (Photo Courtesy Michael Pottie)

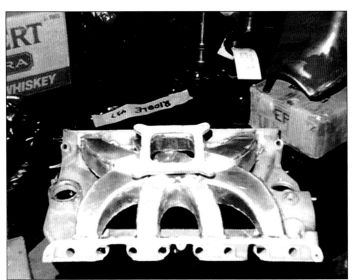

When the factory or the aftermarket doesn't produce an intake of your liking, you build your own. Well, at least that's what Carl Holbrook (and a few others) did in 1976. Holley had an intake out before Carl had the bugs worked out of his fabricated piece. (Photo Courtesy Bob Wytosky)

Carl was notorious for his approach in building winning combinations. He started with a "seasoned" block, one that had miles on it, as any core shifting that was going to happen had already taken place. As boring a 428 was limited to 0.020 to 0.030 over due to the thin walls, Carl turned to replacement sleeves. An added benefit of sleeves is that they extended the life of a good block as, even in 1975, good ones were getting hard to find.

After hot tanking and a thorough cleaning, blocks were Magnafluxed with a focus on the main webbing, which proved to be a weak spot. Carl was meticulous in machining and the way that he assembled his engines. In the same vein as Glidden, who never used an engine stand to assemble an engine, Carl did all machining on his blocks with the motor mounts bolted on and torqued. Also, he replaced the frost plugs with screw-in plugs, feeling that it strengthened the block. Cross-bolt main caps were essential due to the amount of torque the 428 produced.

When it came to camshafts, Carl was developing his own profiles by working with Lunati and later Comp Cams. His later engines were running roller cams with lift upward of 0.775. As for pistons, Bob Duffy was the go-to guy. Carl worked with the manufacturer (as would Glidden) to develop parts to this liking. Carl ran piston-to-wall clearance a loose 0.008 to 0.0085. Rods were shot peened and polished and used the 427 cap-screw bolts.

This is the first of two 1971 Mustangs that Tommy Cooksey campaigned. He purchased this one from a court clerk who used it as her daily driver. (Photo Courtesy Rob Potter)

In the late 1970s, many guys were quitting Super Stock due to several reasons, including changing horsepower factors and changes in index that made it tough to compete. Rules were becoming laxer and the expense in trying to stay competitive was turning Super Stock into a "the one with the most money wins" category.

Carl was one of those who moved away from racing Super Stock during this period. He started building 514 engines based on 460 blocks that were torque monsters. Then, there were the scores of 5.0 Mustangs on which he was installing NOS. Carl never quit racing; he just evolved into other classes and continued to develop new things. Sadly, Carl passed in February 2000.

Tom Cooksey Builds Winners

By the mid-1970s, there were so many great-running Mustangs that it became anyone's guess as to whose car was going to win class at any given event. Tom Cook-sey was one of those you could never count out. Tom started racing a showroom-fresh 1969 Cobra Jet Mustang way back when and with East Coast legend Bob Brown prepping the CJ, he set the SS/H record with an 11.55 at 119.04 mph before building the more familiar Mustang ragtop in 1975.

The convertible was originally a 302-powered car that Tom had torn down and converted to Cobra Jet power. Strict rules of the day had him swapping out everything from the emblems to front springs, to replacing the drum brakes with disks. Tom set and reset the E/S record a half dozen times with the Mustang, running it down to an 11.86 at 115.94 mph. The record stood for two years before the NHRA erased it and set a minimum. Tom found that outside of replacing the bearings every 50 runs or so, the engine and car were a picture of consistency.

Tom went on to build his own engines and developed quite the reputation through his Tom Cooksey's Competition Speed Center. In the late 1970s, he followed the convertible with a pair of 1972 SS/J Mustangs, both powered by the 266-hp Cleveland (big valve, open chamber). The second car was the ex–Bobby Imbody car (Bobby won I/S with the Mustang at the 1977 Sportsnationals) that went through John Lingenfelter and Dale Shannon before Tom made it a class winner. The only issue Tom had with the later Mustang was breaking the $1^3/_8$-inch input shaft on the Toploader. He solved that problem by making the switch to a Doug Nash transmission. Tom retired the Mustang around 1983 and spent the next couple of seasons driving a Pro Gas Pinto. He returned to

Maryland's Tommy Cooksey and his E/S ragtop were a record holder in 1975 with an 11.86 ET at 114.94 mph. The Mustang began life with a 302 before Tommy swapped in the Cobra Jet mill and made it a winner. New owner Gary Cox is driving here. (Photo Courtesy Todd Wingerter)

Dale Shannon, a great friend and partner in crime with Tommy Cooksey, campaigned this 1971 Mustang in 1975 with a Cooksey 429. He had little luck with the combination, so he swapped in a 351 and ran SS/KA. The Mustang originally came through John Lingenfelter. Tommy ended up with the car, painted it white, and ran it with some success with a 351 and 4-speed transmission. (Photo Courtesy Bill Truby)

Mustangs again, building a 1984 model that ran lower Stock classes until he retired in 2005.

1976: Reserving the Celebrations

It was the year of America's Bicentennial, and the Mustang II was in the midst of its five-year cycle. The Mustang remained unchanged, which for the performance minded buyer, was too bad. The largest engine available was the anemic 302, which now carried a 140-hp rating. A new model was introduced in 1975 called the Shadow, which appropriately is where the Mustang II has remained. Records indicate that there has yet to be any Mustang II, regardless of the year, making any mark in Stock or Super Stock. The bodystyle's saving grace was the fact that it was the Ford racer's body of choice in Funny Car and Pro Stock.

Funny Car

Although Don Prudhomme was in the mist of his four consecutive NHRA Funny Car World Championships, there were teams out there that weren't making it easy on him. Right in the thick of the battle were cars campaigned by Shirl Greer, Raymond Beadle, Gary Burgin, and Larry Fullerton. Shirl Greer was runner-up to Prudhomme at the Gatornationals while Gary Burgin defeated the Snake at the U.S. Nationals. Gary also won the IHRA Winter Classic, the Springnationals, Summer-

Lee Hunter campaigned this ex–Bob Glidden, ex–John Dowey Mustang II in 1976 with what some felt was the worst paint job ever to adorn a race car. Lee won the Division 7 Pro Stock title with the car and promised to repaint it for 1977. Don Ness built the chassis. (Photo Courtesy Dan Williams)

The Chicago Patrol Mustang debuted in 1975 with veteran Ron Colson at the controls. Other drivers included Pat Foster and Dale Pulde. The best showing of the Chapman Automotive-sponsored car came at the 1975 IHRA Summer Nationals, where Pat Foster fell in the final to Raymond Beadle. Power came by way of an Ed Pink Hemi. (Photo Courtesy Michael Pottie)

Shirl Greer's one big national event win in 1976 came at the AHRA Gateway Nationals, where he defeated Bob Pickett in Mickey Thompson's Pontiac Grand Am in the final. Shirl won the Division 2 championship that year, and again in 1977 and 1978. (Photo Courtesy Michael Pottie)

nationals, and Southern Nationals. Raymond Beadle once again won the IHRA World Championship after earning victories at the World Nationals, Dixie Nationals, and U.S. Open.

Gary Burgin: The Spoiler

Gary Burgin's IHRA track record, which included wins at the Winter Classic, Spring Nationals, Summer Nationals, and Southern Nationals has been overshadowed by his U.S. Nationals defeat of Don Prudhomme. Prudhomme and his Chevy Monza were on a yearlong win streak, having not lost since falling to the *Blue Max* at the 1975 NHRA U.S. Nationals. Gary Burgin played spoiler this year and erased Prudhomme's hopes of going a full year without a loss.

In 1975, Gary Burgin debuted this new Jaime Sarte-built Mustang and finished second in Funny Car points behind Don Prudhomme. Lacking a major sponsor, he match raced the wheels off the Mustang as a means of supporting his drag racing addiction. (Photo Courtesy Michael Pottie)

Success just seemed to follow Gary Burgin, also known as the Orange Baron, through 1976. That year, he won multiple national events. The nickname came by way of a sponsorship deal he was working on. Although the deal fell through, the name stuck. (Photo Courtesy Michael Pottie)

By no means did Burgin's win come easy. All through qualifying and eliminations, Gary's Mustang trailed Prudhomme by a good tenth of a second. Gary qualified the Mustang down pack with a best of 6.12, while Prudhomme held the number-1 spot with a phenomenal record time of 5.97. Gary meanwhile had laid down the top speed of the meet in the second round when he recorded a time of 238.09. Gary battled on and defeated the previous year's winner Raymond Beadle in the semifinals before facing Prudhomme.

Heading into the final round, Gary had to have been feeling all the pressure as no doubt Prudhomme was the odds-on favorite. Ah, but to the surprise of many, it was the Mustang with the lead off the line. Prudhomme smoked the tires and lost with a 6.46 at 226.70 mph to Gary's 6.25 at 237.46.

Here's to the Little Guys

There was still room for the little guy in Funny Car, but his days were fading fast. Gary Burgin, among many others, was aware of this. Overhead expenses were growing by leaps and bounds, and without deep, *really* deep pockets, or a quality sponsor, you could forget about campaigning a car in the top echelon. In the meantime, a guy could still make it, as match racing was a viable option to support his habit. Of course, with the Funny Car being the fan favorite in the mid-1970s, many tracks hosted shows of 8, 16, and even 64 Funny Cars, and welcomed the lesser-known competition to fill spots.

Pro Stock

The NHRA seemed to change weight breaks as fast as some people changed their socks. The long-wheelbase

Southern California's Jeff Courtie was the epitome of a low-buck Funny Car campaigner, performing all the work on his Mustang himself, including building the chassis. He debuted his first Mustang funny in 1970 after campaigning an Oldsmobile woody wagon in Gas. Jeff retired after the 1978 season. (Photo Courtesy Michael Pottie)

This shot of Dyno Don's Mustang II in a state of disassembly provides a good view as to how the inners of a Pro Stocker looked in 1976. The Don Hardy chassis mounted a four-link suspended 9-inch rear end. (Photo Courtesy Dave Wible)

Wanting something a little different, Pro Stock racer Rick Brantley had Joe Smith Race Cars in Dallas initiate the build of this Shelby Mustang. Rick retired before the car was finished, so the Marriott brothers bought and finished it. They campaigned the Mustang through the 1976 season with a fair amount of success. Relying upon a Gapp & Roush 366-ci Cleveland, driver Bobby Lee Marriott managed times in the 8.60s at 154 mph. (Photo Courtesy Todd Wingerter)

Gardner & Crawford out of Springfield, Virginia, joined the Mustang II march in 1976. The Pro Stocker, seen here at the Springnationals in 1978, was powered by a Cleveland that was built by The Shop in Chester, Virginia. (Photo Courtesy Michael Pottie)

1970 Mustang enjoyed its popularity for about six months before more weight was added making the car less competitive.

Back in vogue were the Pintos and Mustang IIs, but it seemed that the NHRA was doing all it could to put the hurt on the Cleveland-powered cars. It got to the point where both Dyno Don and Scott Shafiroff briefly ran their Pro Stocks in C/Altered, where they at least stood a fighting chance.

New Mustangs were unveiled in 1976 by Dyno, and the team of Gardner & Crawford. Lee Hunter took possession of Bob Glidden's old Don Ness Mustang II and, with an Earl Wade Cleveland, won the Division 7 title.

Bob Glidden was back behind the wheel of his World Championship–winning Pinto. Joining Glidden in a Pinto was the team of Gapp & Roush that had previously seen success with their Mustang II and four-door Maverick.

Although Pro Stock Mustangs made a good showing in division competition and match races, none were able to capture an NHRA, AHRA, or IHRA national event win. It was a rare thing that was rectified in 1977.

Eldon Doman's Rule Changer

Relatively unknown Eldon Doman debuted his Mustang II late in the 1976 season. Pulling the levers on the Lenco for Eldon was former (1964) World Champ Mike Schmidt. Their first national event was the World Finals at Ontario, where Mike qualified but failed to make rounds.

The Mustang initially counted on a Gapp & Roush 331-inch Cleveland for power before Eldon himself built a 377-inch "Clevor" engine, which was a Windsor block with a 400 crank and Cleveland heads. At the time, NHRA weight breaks were based on the block. Using the

Eldon Doman's attractive-looking Mustang II was driven by former world champ Mike Schmidt. The car was built from a body in white and rode on a Don Hardy chassis. (Photo Courtesy Dave Kommel)

No doubt Eldon Doman's Cobra Mustang II is the most original early Pro Stock car in existence, and here's the kicker: he still owns it. (Photo Courtesy Stephen Doman)

Windsor block allowed the Mustang to run at 7.00 lbs/ci as opposed to the 7.30 if he had run a Cleveland. It was a good engine but only ran at one race.

"Right before the finals, a Chevy mob came to the trailer with NHRA officials demanding to see the engine," Eldon's son Stephen said. "[The] NHRA changed the rules before the final round, and from then on weight breaks were applied to Cleveland heads, so they had to add weight. As Mike went to stage the car, the throw-out bearing seized and ate the fingers off the pressure plate, causing the car to creep through the starting beams and red light."

Here's a funny story from the World Finals: Tech didn't want to pass the Mustang because it didn't have a headliner. Mike had a stack of those famous Farrah Fawcett pictures, so he taped them to the inside of the roof. Although the Mustang never garnered a lot of attention, it qualified at every race it entered. Its biggest win came at a Pro Stock bash at Tucson. The best times for the car before it was retired in 1980 was an 8.55 at 162 mph.

Rick Auxier Does Super Modified

Ford's greatest threat in Super Modified was the Mustang of Rick Auxier. The Cleveland-powered car had numerous class wins under its belt. Sam Auxier Jr. gets credit for helping to make the car a winner. (Photo Courtesy Sam Auxier Jr.)

Super Modified was a category dreamed up back in 1974 by *Car Craft* magazine writers Rick Voegelin and John Dianna. The idea was an inexpensive, heads-up Sportsman category, which they sold to the NHRA and debuted at the 1975 Winternationals.

Super Modified initially consisted of just one class, which was designated A/SM. The rules were basic. Cars could be no older than 1967, a minimum of 9 lbs/ci was required, and the maximum engine size was 366 ci. Racers were limited to a single carburetor no larger than 750 cfm.

With the NHRA expanding the Super Modified class into three in 1976, Rick's Mustang moved down to B/SM with its weight break being 9.50 to 10.49 lbs/ci. (Photo Courtesy Sam Auxier Jr.)

Minor porting of the heads to match the gaskets was allowed. Cars could weigh no less than 2,850 pounds with no more than 50 percent of the weight on the rear wheels. Rear tire width was kept to a maximum of 10.5 inches.

The class looked great on paper, but in short order it was swamped with first-gen Camaros and early Novas. One of the few Fords making a dent in the category was the 1970 Mustang of Rick Auxier.

Rick's Mustang was an original Boss 429 car that was handed down to him by his older brother Sam. Rick ran the car for a few years in SS/C with the Boss engine before jumping into Super Modified in 1975. The Boss was pulled and, in its place, went a 351 built by Rick with a hand from Sam. Rules prohibited the Boss 429 cars from running Super Modified, as the Kar-Kraft modified shock towers were rejected. Rick solved the problem by robbing a junkyard Mustang of its towers and welding them in place of the Kar-Kraft towers. In doing so, Rick "found" a couple of extra inches on each side of the engine. It was a little something

Stocks and Super Stocks

In Super Stock, rules now allowed vehicle weight to be shifted 75 pounds over or under the factory shipping weight so that cars could fit the class better, although the variance wasn't allowed to move a car up or down a class. The same rule went into effect for Stock class cars in 1977. Further rule changes allowed for rear floor pans from the front spring eye through to the trunk to be narrowed to make room for the accepted narrowed rear ends. The tire size rule changed as well stating that they must be 14.5x33 when new.

Further rule changes in Super Stock allowed for the removal of the heater, wipers, and sway bars. Driver weight was now added to the car, adding 170 pounds to curb weight. Winners in Stocks and Super Stocks? We had them in numbers during the 1976 season.

no one seemed to pick up on.

Another item that no one seemed to notice were the "tongues" that ran out of each primary tube into the exhaust port. Essentially, this raised the floor of the port. Backing the Cleveland was a Hays clutch and 2.78 first-gear Toploader transmission. A sticking point for a few racers was the hydraulic clutch Sam used, something tech never had a problem with. All they cared was that the pedals were in the stock location.

With Rick's father having shares in Doug Nash Enterprises, he did some testing of the Nash 4+1 for the company. Rick ran the transmission one year as a 4-speed and could get as high as a 3.05 first gear. Completing the driveline was a 9-inch rear with 5.86 gears controlled by a pair of 32-inch ladder bars.

Rick Auxier's 1970 Boss 429 Mustang was raced in SS/C from 1971 to 1974, then converted to 351C power to run Super Modified from 1975 to 1977. Rick won four NHRA national events running A/SM. (Photo Courtesy Sam Auxier Jr.)

In Rick's first national event, the 1975 Springnationals, he defeated the Jegs-sponsored Chevy II of Larry Nelson in the final. After the run, the cars were weighed with the Chevy going first. First, the front half was weighed, and then the car pulled forward to weigh the back half. The Chevy passed with no problem, so Larry pulled ahead and waited to see if the Mustang was okay. Being weighed with the driver, Rick would adjust the seat back or forward, depending on which end was being weighed. It was something a few racers did. The Chevy passed with no problem, so Larry pulled ahead and waited to see if the Mustang was okay.

The move didn't help Rick this time, as the Mustang proved to be light on the front and overweight on the back. Rick had been having problems with his battery dying, so he swapped the larger battery from his tow rig into the Mustang. Well, the replacement battery was about twice the size of the battery Rick originally had in the car. The added weight threw off the balance. At this point, the weigh manager, who happened to be the brother of Gasser legend Ricky Barratt (C/Gas Pinto), who worked at a Ford dealership, waved Larry on, telling him, "He's good." He then turned to Rick and said, "You're not good front to back. Go fix it."

Although the Mustang never held the class record, times in the mid-10s won Rick not only the Springnationals in 1975 but also the Summernationals in 1976 and the Sportsnationals in 1977 and 1978. In 1979, he purchased his brother Sam's old Pro Stock 1971 Mustang and used the Cleveland from the Super Modified Mustang to power the car in D/Gas.

The older Mustangs remained a popular choice in the lower Stock and Super Stock classes. Hired gun Paul Dilcher hopped in Gary Williams's 1965 Mustang at the 1976 NHRA Winternationals and came within a hair of winning SS/OA. Gary had more than his share of success with the record-holding Mustang, as well as an SS/MA 1964 Comet that he ran in conjunction with his brother Bill. (Photo Courtesy Dave Kommel)

Jeff Velde began racing in 1970 with this meadowlark yellow 1969 Super Cobra Jet Mustang. Jeff ran the best of parts that helped move the Mustang to low-11 ETs. He raced the car until 1975, when he purchased the Brandon & Turnage Mustang. (Photo Courtesy "Hot Rod" Tommy Shaw)

Dave Moreno had raced his Mustang for years before winning his first national event. In 1985, while campaigning the car as a D/Stocker, he won the World Finals. Twenty-three years and 11 months later, he won the NHRA Sportsnationals at Fontana with the Mustang. He also won D/S at the 1984 Winternationals. Here, in 1976, he was runner-up in class at the Winternationals. (Photo Courtesy Dave Kommel)

The SS/F Mustang of Jeff Velde launched like no other. Jeff counted on a small crew to keep the Mustang going. His wife, Patty, helped a lot and was one of the first to stand on the start line, recording competitors' times. (Photo Courtesy Michael Pottie)

Jeff Velde

How do you take a car as successful as the *Nitro 9* Mustang of Brandon & Turnage and make it better? Well, apparently, the trick was to sell it to Jeff Velde.

Jeff took possession of the Mustang at the end of the 1975 season and spent 1976 winning nearly everything possible: the Winternationals, Gatornationals, Springnationals, Sportsnationals, and Indy. Jeff was a natural behind the wheel. In total, he had 16 national event class wins and set 13 class records. He closed the 1976 season by setting the class record in October with a 10.47 at 130.43 mph, which was a record that stood well into 1977. Of course, like any success in life, he had to earn it.

Jeff was a sales manager at Pekin, Illinois, Velde Ford in 1969 when he sold an SCJ Mustang to an eager customer. Within months, the owner returned with the Mustang, wanting to trade it in because he had lost his license and was looking for something a little more subdued. Jeff had just the car for him, his wife's Mustang convertible. Jeff whipped home, and without his wife's knowledge, sold her car to the gentleman.

Jeff retained the meadowlark yellow Mustang and raced it for the next four years, turning a best of 11-flat times before purchasing the Brandon & Turnage Mustang. Slick Thurman pulled the wrenches for Velde, who was a great driver but was initially limited in his mechanical skills. Like all of us, though, he learned as he went.

Help came from Bob Glidden and Gene Turnage, and later, engines came with the help of Carl Holbrook and Jim Bates. Velde's main crew at the track was his wife and two daughters when they came of age. Bates did a lot of machine work on the engines and when Jeff went Pro Stock racing in the 1980s, Bates teamed with him. The SS/F Mustang ran a best of 10.28 in 1980 with a Carl Holbrook Cobra Jet. Carl and Jeff made use of only proven parts including Canadian heads (Jeff had six sets), side-bolted block with replacement sleeves, and a Keith Wilson–fabricated intake.

Jeff was in the process of building a four-link Mustang when the opportunity came to buy Bob Glidden's stars and stripes Pro Stock Pinto. Jeff sold the Mustangs to make the buy. He ran the Pinto in B/FX and won Comp Eliminator at the Cajun Nationals 1981 with it. The Pinto was followed by a run in Pro Stock where he partnered with both Bates and later Buddy Ingersoll. Jeff closed his career behind the wheel of a Super Stock Shelby Mustang where he won his class with it at Indy in 2005 and 2006.

Jim Morgan: If You Can't Beat Them . . .

For Jim Morgan, running a 396-powered 1968 Camaro in SS/EA back in 1969 got old quick. Jim's problem was that he was continu-

Jim Morgan's CJ Mustang held the SS/GA record in June 1976 with an 11.02 ET, later lowering it to a 10.86 at 124.82 mph. Jim, in action here at the 1976 World Finals, campaigned the Mustang for two years, beginning in 1975. (Photo Courtesy Dave Kommel)

Jeff Velde ran his Mustang in SS/E and SS/F and held records through 1979 when he ran a 10.30 ET. He won his class at the 1976 Winternationals as well as class at the U.S. Nationals in 1975 and 1976. (Photo Courtesy Rob Potter)

ously being hammered in class by Cobra Jet Mustangs. In 1970, the LaPlata, Maryland, resident decided to do something about it: he cashed in the Camaro for a 1969 CJ Mustang of his own.

Jim picked up the candy-apple red Mach 1 for $1,400 after the owner ventilated the block. The gentleman had purchased the Mustang from Dorsey Gray Ford in Prince Fredrick, Maryland, a dealership located about 40 miles from LaPlata. With nothing to lose, Jim headed to the dealership in hopes of landing a sponsorship deal.

Jim Morgan tried a 4-speed for a while but went back to the C-6 after a Toploader came apart on him. Jim set and reset NHRA class records 18 times as well as another half dozen times in IHRA competition. (Photo Courtesy Rob Potter)

This Mustang was an original 1970 Boss 302 car that Jim converted to a 1969 Cobra Jet car. It carries the Division 1 championship number that Jim won in 1976. He campaigned this one through 1979. (Photo Courtesy Michael Pottie)

The dealer proved to be more than receptive to the idea and the sponsorship ended up lasting 12 years. It was a good deal where the dealer supplied parts and in 1973 a tow rig, which Jim's partner at the time, Dickie Estevez, turned into a ramp truck. The 428 that powered the Mustang went together with the help of Kline Automotive in Richmond, Maryland.

Jim eventually campaigned five different Mustangs. The original Mach I gave way to an R-code convertible, which Jim used to win the Division 1 Super Stock title in 1974. Jim ran the ragtop with a 4-speed in 1973, but when the case split, he installed a C-6.

Jim had fond memories of that first division title. Heading into the final points meet of the season at Atco, New Jersey, he was 200 points behind the team of Bennett & Sirianni, who ran a killer SS/I Camaro. Lady luck had Sirianni fall in the second round, and Jim went on to win the meet and take the title.

A new Mustang was built for 1975, an SS/GA 1969 R-code fastback, which Jim took to the World Finals in 1976 after winning another division championship. By this point, Jim was building his own engines and doing a fine job of it. Initially, he had the usual oiling issues affecting bearings. He recalled friends teasing him because at the end of each race day he'd have the car in the shop to check the bearings in preparation for the next day's racing.

The cross-bolted block counted on a good oiling system, proper clearances, attention to detail, and precision to stay alive. Under the 735 Holley was an unusual intake, an Offenhauser Port-O-Sonic, which Jim swears by to this day. Jim campaigned the Mustang into 1977, winning class through those years at a couple of national events (1975 Summernationals and 1977 Gatornationals) and the division championship in 1976. While campaigning the car, Jim set the SS/GA record at 11.13 and took it down to a 10.86 before he retired the car.

Looking to get an edge, Jim built a new car in 1977 that took full advantage of the rules. He converted an original 1970 Boss 302 Mustang to a 1969 and ran it in SS/GA with a Cobra Jet. It was a pretty trick car, which carried a 12-bolt Chevy rear end and Mopar Super Stock springs and pinion snubber.

Why the Chevy rear? At the time there was a rumor circulating that due to the angle of the ring and pinion gear there was better roll resistance. Jim noticed that fellow Super Stock racer Jim Kinnett ran a 12-bolt under his Hemi Mopar and figured he'd give it a try. Whether it made a difference or not, Jim never really knew, as it was a whole new car.

Up front, the usual modifications were made to loosen the suspension. Further changes included cut and welded A-arms that helped to retain proper wheel angle through suspension travel.

A C-6 with a Marv Ripes convertor backed the Cobra Jet. Unlike today's modifications that allow C-6 transmissions to be fitted with Chrysler 727 inners (and worth 2 tenths), you only had stock stuff to work with back then. The 12-bolt rear was fitted with upward of 5.57 gears. Jim raced this car through 1979 and once again ran record times and won national events.

His final Mustang was a 1968 CJ car that he built in 1981 and ran 10.30s before teaming up with Joe Clark in 1983 to run Pro Stock with an ex–*Grumpy's Toy* Camaro. Jim returned in the mid-1990s to campaign a B/SA 1969 Mustang with his son. They won numerous events together before Jim retired in 1998. In total, he had set 18 NHRA class records and another half dozen IHRA records with his string of Mustangs.

Scott Main: NHRA Stock World Champ

Today, Scott Main is better known for the success he had competing in the Engine Masters series, as well as the business he established in 1979 and operates to this day, Cam Research. However, back in 1976, the Colorado resident was just a 20-year-old kid fulfilling a dream that first took root in the 1960s.

Scott began drag racing in 1969 at age 14 behind the wheel of his own Super Cobra Jet Mustang. Yes, you read that right, his own SCJ Mustang! Scott saved up for the down payment from his paper route and then begged and pleaded with his parents to co-sign the loan. He managed to convince them that he could swing the required $50 a month payment with money earned from his paper route. Reluctantly, his parents caved and agreed to sign for the car.

Too young to drive on the street, Scott had his mom drive him to the track where he raced the C-6-equipped Mustang in Pure Stock.

"Track officials just assumed I was of age and never asked how old I was," Scott said.

Scott built a good engine for the car in 1973 and ran Stock Eliminator. By 1974, 18-year-old Scott had done so

well with the Mustang that he won the Division 5 points championship. In 1975, he ran the same combination and was runner-up in his division. Scott felt things changed in 1975, as Winston hooked up with the NHRA.

"We went from running for $300 and a trophy to racing for $1,200," he said. "Things got a lot more serious, and I felt I needed to build a new car."

Not wanting to add a cage and modify the Super Cobra Jet car, Scott searched for a new car. He found one

It's hard to believe, but Scott Main, at 14 years old, bought this SCJ Mustang new with paper route money. His parents cosigned, and his mother drove the car to the racetrack for him. "I raced it in Pure Stock initially, and they never asked my age," Scott said. He hung onto the Mustang all these years and has restored it. (Photo Courtesy James Smart)

At one time, Colorado was just as well known for its drag racing as it was for its skiing. Scott Main frequented most of the state's tracks through the 1970s and worked hard for his division titles. (Photo Courtesy Bill Ringer)

A picture of consistency. It seems that Scott Main was a natural. Like many, he thanks his older brother for instilling in him an interest in drag racing. (Photo Courtesy James Smart)

The sedate-looking Cobra Jet coupe of Scott Main surprised many people. Although it was a division-winning world championship car, Scott stated that it never got a lot of ink because it didn't have a fancy paint job. (Photo Courtesy Steve Goddard)

in the form of an original 1968 Cobra Jet coupe (1 of 50 produced). A neighbor owned the car and had blown the engine street racing. Scott handed over $350 for the car and set to work.

Scott debuted the C/S coupe in the spring of 1976 at a division race and won it. It was another great season for Scott, who won his second Division 5 title and earned an invitation to the World Finals. There, the Mustang ran consistent 11.60 times as Scott battled his way to the final round in Stock. In the final, he faced the I/SA Dodge of fellow Denver resident Ron Peters. Ron took the handicap start but lost, running too fast as he attempted to hold off the Mustang's 11.67. For his efforts, Scott took home bragging rights and a cool $12,000.

Building his own engines, Scott counted on Verle Stevens to perform the machine work. Scott stated that he had no real issues with his combination, outside of oiling and bearings, which he finally worked through. It helped that Stock rules limited valve-spring pressure to 90 pounds closed and 290

open. With shimmed valves, you could only rev 5,900 to 6,000 rpm before you floated the intake valves. You just couldn't hurt the engine at those RPM. Peak power came around 5,500 rpm.

In 1977, Scott once again was runner-up in Division 5. He was 20 years old and figuring it was time to start thinking about a career. No illusions of grandeur here, Scott knew he was only going to go so far in the sport. He accomplished what he wanted and retired after the U.S. Nationals in 1977. He sold the Mustang and helped the new owner transform the car into a Super Stocker. The Mustang won class at the U.S. Nationals in 1978 and played runner-up at the Mile High Nationals in 1979.

1977: Only One Way to Go

Stripes, stickers, and flares sold new cars in 1977, and the Mustang II was no exception. Although sales hit bottom in 1977 with a little over 153,000 units sold, the Mustang still led its field. The hard-core drag racers saw through the gimmicks and stuck with what won them races. While the older Mustangs continued to hammer on the competition in Stock and Super Stock, the Mustang II was taking Pro Stock by storm, despite the less-than-favorable weight breaks.

This is proof that not all competitive Pro Stock Mustangs in 1977 were of the Mustang II variety. Larry Sengstack purchased Bob Glidden's 1970 Mustang Pro Stocker and rebodied it as a 1973 Mustang. Larry debuted his American Flyer *in 1977 and campaigned it with a Cleveland mill developed with the help of Scott Shafiroff. In 1979, the car was rebodied as a Fairmont. (Photo Courtesy Bob Snyder)*

Funny Car

Wins were few and far between for the Mustang through 1977, but it wasn't from a lack of trying. Raymond Beadle who returned with his World Championship–winning *Blue Max* was runner-up to Prudhomme at the NHRA Winternationals in February. In June, he won the AHRA Gateway Nationals by defeating John Collins in Tom McEwen's Plymouth Duster. Johnny White, who seemingly came out of nowhere with his John Buttera–built Mustang, soloed for a win at the NHRA Cajun Nationals after the Camaro of Billy Meyer fell to mechanical issues.

The Chi-Town Hustler team, well known for their smokie burnouts and a long line of Dodge Funny Cars, placed itself in a Mustang during 1977 after striking up a sponsorship deal with Dave Cory Ford of Naperville, Illinois. A runner-up finish at the IHRA U.S. Open came in 1977 before major wins with driver Denny Savage followed in 1978 at the IHRA Pro-Am Nationals, Northern Nationals, and the NHRA Summernationals.

Bunny Business

Carol "Bunny" Burkett, the First Lady of Funny Car, graduated from a Pro Stock Pinto to a Top Alcohol Mustang II in 1976. Bunny began racing in 1964 behind the wheel of a Stock class Mustang. She followed with a 1968 Mustang in Super Stock through 1972 and was a participant on the Miss Universe Drag Team. It was a team of women drivers that

Carol "Bunny" Burkett ran a Top Alcohol Funny Car beginning in 1976 with this Logghe-chassied Bunny Burkett Mustang II. She saw her greatest success running the same class in the 1980s. Carol picked up the "Bunny" nickname after working early in life at the Playboy mansion in Baltimore. (Photo Courtesy Michael Pottie)

According to the website 70sfunnycars.com, in 1975, Arnie Karp and Keith Hughes joined forces with Comp racers Bob Ellison and Rick McGarvey to form Yankee Racing. Their accumulated effort was the Boston Strangler, *a BB/FC Mustang. A new S&W Race Cars* Boston Strangler *appeared here in 1977 and launched the team on its winning ways. The* Boston Strangler *ran Nick Boninfante's Fuel Funny Car circuit that year and won 6 of the 14 races it attended. Power came by way of a 517-ci Donovan Hemi. (Photo Courtesy Michael Pottie)*

Something that had the Chrysler fraternity crying in their Corn Flakes was the site of the Chi-Town Hustler *name on a Mustang. With Denny Savage at the wheel, the team saw a fair amount of success. (Photo Courtesy Michael Pottie)*

was dreamed up by promoter Tom "Smoker" Smith that toured Northeast tracks through the early 1970s.

In 1973, Bunny began racing Pro Stock with her unforgettable pink *Lil Cotton Bunny* Pinto. With a desire to go faster, she joined the Top Alcohol Funny Car ranks in 1976, when she purchased the Vindicator Mustang II. Although Bunny ran a Chrysler Hemi in the car, the previously owner, Drake Viscome, had campaigned the Mustang with a Boss 429.

With her good looks, infectious smile, and a drive to win, Bunny gained a following as she toured the Mustang up and down the East Coast. Her greatest success came in the 1980s behind the wheel of a Top Alcohol Dodge Laser, but to many her exploits in the Mustangs were the times to remember.

Iowa-based Dave Shafer joined the party when he debuted his Mustang II in 1977. Dave focused his attention on AHRA races and circuit races, where he did pretty well for himself. Power came by way of a 357-ci Cleveland engine. (Photo Courtesy Ron Berges)

Pro Stock

The category was a nightmare due to the weight breaks and everybody knew it. There were 22 different breaks, and no combination carried more weight than a Cleveland-powered Ford (7.10 to 7.20 lbs/ci). Even Chrysler's Hemi cars carried less weight, and still they complained and boycotted NHRA competition. Ford racers battled on, and no one showed more determination than Dyno Don, whose efforts paid off big-time.

Steve Davis and John Sain got in on the "old is new again" thing when they debuted their 1970 Mustang in 1976. Under the hood was a 302 that propelled Steve to low-9 ETs. The chassis for this one was built by Joe Smith. The Mustang later ran Pro Gas. (Photo Courtesy Dave Kommel)

Mustang's First Pro Stock World Title

Pro Stock in 1977 turned out to be the year of the Mustang II, as no less than five of the cars competed in the top echelon of the category. Lee Hunter started the year right by defeating the Mustang II of Dyno Don at the season-opening AHRA Winternationals at Bee Line. It's a shame that it was Lee's only career national event victory.

Dyno, on the other hand, won the NHRA Pro Stock title in 1977, the first of four Pro Stock World Titles that Ford's Mustang earned. The other three were won by IHRA competitors: Ronnie Sox won the title in 1981 and Rickie Smith won it in 1982 and 1986.

Nicholson and Crew Chief Jon Kaase put a concerted effort forward to win the NHRA Pro Stock crown in 1977. To get the job done, Don counted on a 340-inch Cleveland (4.08 bore and 3.25 stroke). When it came to money-generating match races, an aluminum Cleveland measuring 392 inches did the job.

At the season-opening NHRA Winternationals Don made it to the final round before falling to a red light against Larry Lombardo in Grumpy Jenkins Monza. Dyno made it clear, though, that he meant business, having held the number-1 qualifying position with an 8.72.

The tables turned at the following Gatornationals, where Don defeated Lombardo in the semifinals. As told in *National Dragster*, the semifinal round was "for all practical purposes" the final round. While Wally Booth won

At the end of 1977, Don Nicholson held the best win-loss record of all three pro-category leaders. Here, at the Fallnationals, Don was handed one of his few losses of the season. (Photo Courtesy Larry Pfister).

At the next two races, the Springnationals and the Summernationals, Don exchanged wins with Frank Iaconio, beating the Chevy Monza at the Springnationals and losing in the semifinals at the Summernationals. Don had set the Pro Stock record in the second round at the Summernationals with an 8.57 but hurt his good motor in the following round. Facing Iaconio with his back-up motor, Dyno lost with a quicker 8.67 to Iaconio's 8.75.

It's hard to believe that with the amount of success Don had throughout his career, it took until 1977 before he won his first NHRA Nationals. The victory came in convincing fashion, starting with Don setting the low ET of the meet with an 8.61 and finishing with him defeating two-time World Champ Bob Glidden and his Pinto.

the other semifinal match, he blew the engine in his Hornet and was unable to make repairs in time for the final call. The Nicholson-Jenkins semi match saw Lombardo foul on the line, handing the win to Don, who took it with an 8.74 at 157.34 mph.

Like at the Winternationals, Don held the number-1 qualifying position, recording an 8.65. He also took low ET and top speed of the meet with an 8.64 at 157.61 mph, which gave him an early season lead in the Pro Stock points standings.

In between, Don and the Mustang II eliminated a red-lighting Warren Johnson in the second round and in the semifinals, defeated Larry Lombardo, who was driving the borrowed Monza of Ronnie Manchester. Lombardo lost the Grumpy's Toy Monza after blowing a tire during qualifying. The Monza hit the rail, and an ensuing fire left him without a ride. In the final round, Don took the lead against an ailing Glidden and took the win with an 8.74 at 154.10 mph. The win all but guaranteed Don the World Championship.

The same Indy weekend, Don was awarded the coveted *Car Craft* magazine Ollie Award, recognizing his contribution and impact on the sport throughout his career. Chief wrench Jon Kaase meanwhile joined an elite crowd when S-K Tools welcomed him to its Hall of Fame.

In the nine NHRA national events, Don and the Mustang II ran in 1977, he qualified number-1 three times, number-2 four times, number-3 once, and number-4 once. In regional points meets, he qualified number-1 at all of them.

"Our closest competitor was Larry Lombardo in Jenkins's car," Dyno said in a *Super Stock & Drag Illustrated* interview. "They had won the championship the year before."

Jon Kaase and Don Nicholson performed well in late 1976 and put forward a concerted effort to pursue the NHRA championship in 1977. More times than not, Kaase could be seen guiding the Mustang through the burnout box. Legal weight times in the 8.60s were the norm. (Photo Courtesy Michael Pottie)

Don took strategic measures to hold Lombardo at bay.

"I had already won my allotted number of divisional points races but went to the last one [that] Lombardo ran and beat him early in eliminations to keep him from winning any points," Dyno said.

Well played, Don. Well played.

Stocks and Super Stocks

Category rules saw some changes of significance. In Super Stock, replacement 2x3 rear frame rails were allowed for the first time, as well as aftermarket 4-speed transmissions. Roll bars were now required in cars running SS/A through SS/HA. In Stock, aftermarket valve springs were now allowed, as long as they had the same appearance as stock (ie: single spring, damper).

Horsepower factors in 1977 for the 428 were as follows: In Stock, the 1968 428 with dished pistons and heavy valves was now rated by the NHRA at 365 hp. The 1969 428 with non–Ram Air and dished pistons was factored to 355 hp. The 1969 Ram Air dished pistons 428 carried a 365-hp rating, and the 1970 428 non–Ram Air was factored to 355 hp, while the Ram Air-equipped cars were adjusted to 365.

Clyde Birch's 1967 Mustang (disguised as a 1968) held the C/SA record briefly in 1977 with an 11.32 ET. Powering the Mustang was a Minnesota Auto Specialist-built 428 Cobra Jet. (Photo Courtesy Robert Paul)

Marcel Cloutier continued to shine, teaming here in 1977 with Norm Nevin and Steve Steele. Cloutier won the Division 7 Stock championship in 1976. (Photo Courtesy Dave Kommel)

Winter Fun

The Winternationals was a great indication as to the kind of year it was going to be for the Mustang and their owners. In Super Stock stick, the Northwest's Jeff Wittig won SS/F in his 1968 CJ Mustang, and Bob Hester won SS/H in his CJ-powered 1969 Mustangs. In Super Stock auto, the early Mustangs were still kicking it as Gary Williams took SS/PA honors with his 289-powered 1965. Oklahoma's Lloyd Bray, who was always a threat, repeated his 1976 Winternationals SS/FA class win with his 1968 Mustang when he defeated the Chevelle of George Stassi with a 10.98.

Ricky Whittinghill in the Mustang of Tom Duarll was always a tough competitor. Based out of Central City, Kentucky, the Mustang ran both SS/H and SS/I. Although major event victory escaped the pair, it did show well in divisional races and a few national events. (Photo Courtesy Bill Truby)

Lloyd Bray

Bray followed his Winternationals win with class wins at the Sportsnationals and Indy. Bray's Mustang was originally campaigned by Gas Ronda and was one of the original lightweights. Ronda sold the Mustang to Leo Roy after the Winternationals, who then sold it to Bray in 1971. Bray and partner Don (DG) Gillam gained quite the reputation for themselves operating Precision Performance in Bartlesville, Oklahoma.

The pair went into business in 1970 and can be credited for having their hands on many class winners. They campaigned their Mustang through 1983, seeing their fair share of success before replacing the car with an SS/GT Mustang. As happens with most of these factory drag cars, the 1968 has been restored back to its Gas Ronda appearance.

Threatt & Johnson

In Stock, the big news was Chad Johnson driving the H/SA 1972 Mustang of Joe Threatt to the Winternationals Eliminator win by defeating the G/S Fairlane of John Dusenbery in the final round with a 12.58 at 93.93 mph. Chad, one of the Wilson Ford Drag Club members, had built his reputation in bracket racing. He met Joe Threatt through engine builder Steve Steele. Joe originally lived in Illinois and had Southern California–based Steele build him a 1969 CJ Mustang convertible in 1974. Steve delivered the car to Joe at the Sportsnationals and took E/SA class. In 1975, Joe relocated to Whittier where he opened an Aamco Transmission shop.

Lloyd Bray and partner Don Gillam saw a lot of success with their lightweight Mustang. After selling the Ford-itude fastback, the pair campaigned a Cobra Jet-powered Fox Body Mustang. (Photo Courtesy Michael Pottie)

Steve Steele drove this E/SA Mustang for Joe Threatt in 1977. The Cobra Jet convertible could run high-11 ETs all day. (Photo Courtesy Dave Kommel)

Joe Threatt supplied the car that 19-year-old Chad Langdon drove to a Winternationals Stock Eliminator win. By this time, Chad had already established a reputation around Southern California as a good, consistent driver. (Photo Courtesy Dave Kommel)

The Winternationals-winning Mustang ran both as a 1971 and a 1972 model as the variance in horsepower ratings between the two years made it an easy switch between classes. After the Winternationals win, Joe gave 19-year-old Chad the green light to take the car out on tour.

Chad headed east, racing the car for about six months before the money ran out. Along the way, Chad played runner-up in class at the Sportsnationals and set the class speed record with a 108.67 mph.

According to Chad, what woke the 351 was the Clay Smith camshaft. In Stock, where a builder was limited by rules, the cam's ramp speed and timing were the only areas that could be played with. Threatt ran a Bobby Thompson (formerly of Rossi transmission) torque convertor in the C-6, while out back the 9-inch rear end usually carried 5:13 gears. Best of times for the car were 12.0s at 113 mph.

Johnson & Novak

It was Bob Glidden who recommended the convertible to Bob Johnson, as you could run the car at the same weight as a hardtop but in a class lower. In the 1970s, you couldn't tie the sub-frames together, so the convertible had the advantage as they came from the factory tied.

Joe Novak was Bob's partner and built the motors for the non-original R-code Mustang. The pair worked at Rosen-Novak Ford (no relation) who applied the fancy paint in 1975. Joe Novak was a line mechanic while Bob was the service manager. The convertible was the number-1 qualifier at almost every race it attended. Between races, they pulled the motor and replaced rings and bearings. Eventually the pair figured out the oiling issues and rerouted restricted oil flow. They also added a windage tray.

Behind the Cobra Jet ran a reworked Toploader. Depending on the track or conditions they ran different-weight flywheels. The custom rear's mono-leaf suspension worked in similar fashion to today's Calvert leaf springs and operated with no track bars or pinion snubber. To aid weight transfer, the pair went to the extent of drilling out the left front shock. Johnson managed to record 11.80 times in 1977.

The pair switched to racing a 1970 Cobra Jet Mustang, doing so into the 1980s. They later went with a 1967 Mustang powered by a 390. The weak top end (valve springs) meant the car couldn't rev and saw limited success. Rules changes in 1990 allowed racers to run any valve spring.

Rainero's Return

Tony Rainero returned to action in 1977 with a Cleveland-powered I/Stock 1971 Mustang convertible that left many competitors scratching their heads. Lim-

Colorado's Bob Johnson took Bob Glidden's advice back in 1973 and built this 1969 Cobra Jet convertible. Marcel Cloutier built the motor that moved the car to numerous wins and records. The beautiful paint was done by Rosen-Novak Ford. (Photo Courtesy Dave Kommel)

Tony Rainero campaigned this 1971 Mustang with great success in I/S between 1977 and 1980, taking class wins at Indy and the Sportsnationals. The convertible had a two-piece rear window. Tony cut a razor-thin slit through the middle the rear window to relieve the pressure that built up within the car at speed to prevent the roof from ballooning. No one ever caught on. (Photo Courtesy William Bozgan)

Tony Rainero's Mustang was campaigned as a 1972 model. Note the Ram Air, which was only available on the 2-barrel-equipped Cleveland in 1972. As Tony recalled, Ford's Bruce Sizemore put out a technical bulletin on the Ram Air setup for the 4-barrel-equipped Cobra Jet and thought it was funny that the NHRA accepted it without question and didn't impose a horsepower limit. (Photo Courtesy William Bozgan)

Bill Bozgan, pictured here with his wife in front of their Detroit home, purchased the Mustang from Rainero after he quit racing it in 1980. Bill, like Tony, had worked for Ford and lent a hand to Tony when he raced the car. The Mustang has been restored by Bill and put back on the street. (Photo Courtesy William Bozgan)

ited by rules that dictated a stock valvetrain, your typical Cleveland-powered Stocker was limited to approximately 5,500 to 5,800 rpm. Magically, Tony managed to get an extra 1,500 rpm out of his Cleveland, which seemed to make power upward of 7,500 rpm.

When first built, Tony took the Cleveland to Don Bowles's shop to run it on his dyno, rather than to a local dyno, as a means of keeping it away from prying eyes. Once on the dyno, Tony had Don run the engine up in increments, finally reaching 7,500 rpm before Don decided to take a break. Stunned by the numbers he was seeing, Don's break consisted of getting Jack Roush down to the shop to see what was going on. Don and Jack both knew that engine combination should not have been able to rev that high. By the time Don

returned with Jack in tow, Tony had the engine off the dyno and loaded on his truck. He wasn't about to share his little secret with anyone. And Jack? Well, he fully understood.

Tony accomplished the feat by getting shorter pushrods and special shims (in thousandths of an inch) for under the rocker arms, which were not easily visible. He did each valve separately and brought the hydraulic lifter plunger to within 0.005 of being fully extended. This basically made the lifter act as a solid lifter, but at teardown it still looked like a regular hydraulic lifter.

The modifications allowed Tony to make better use of the large Cleveland ports. His reward came in the form of a class record and a win at Indy in 1977, when he defeated the Camaro of Wayne Shaw with a 12.53 at 108.56 mph. He set the class record in April of 1979 with a 12.11 at 110.97 mph and ran a best of 11.84.

1978: Encore! Encore!

It was the final year for the Mustang II, and outside of a few dress-up models, nothing changed. Although it is bashed by the Mustang pursuits, you can say the 1974–1978 Mustang II was the right car for the time. Styling-wise it wasn't a bad-looking car. The fastback body remained a popular choice in Pro Stock, but weight breaks continued to hammer on the Mustang II and Cleveland combination.

Debuting his Mustang in 1978 was up-and-comer Rickie Smith. He spent part of the year working out the bugs before winning his first race in 1979. Rickie counted on a Gapp & Roush big-inch Boss to record one of Pro Stock's first 7-second times. (Photo Courtesy Mike Dimery)

John Turley hailed from Sherman, Texas, and was a tough competitor. In 1971, he won the Division 4 Super Stock title, and over the years, he kept right on winning. John is seen here at Hallsville Drag Strip in 1978 running an IHRA race. (David Mecey Photo, Courtesy Robert Kornegay)

Funny Car

The face of AA/FC was changing in 1978. Match races were drying up as the expense to track owners to bring in a couple of cars was cutting too deeply into the profits. Many budget-minded teams felt the loss as the match race dates had been keeping them afloat. Simple economics, but when the dates dried up, so did the teams.

Big wins for the Mustang dwindled after 1978, save for notable wins by Gary Burgin in both 1979 and 1980. In the meantime, 1978 was a notable year. In IHRA competition, Denny Savage and the Chi-Town Hustler crew were cleaning house, and Raymond Beadle returned with his Mustang to win both the AHRA and NHRA World Finals. The year brought a sense of finality as in 1979 both the *Chi-Town Hustler* and Beadle's *Blue Max* ran Chrysler bodies.

Bob Anderson and Russ Osley debuted this Hemi-powered BB/FC Mustang II in 1978 as the Kop Kar. Sponsored by Sloan Ford in Downington, Pennsylvania, the Mustang was renamed Wind & Fire in 1979 and continued to be an East Coast threat in Top Alcohol. (Photo Courtesy Ed Aigner)

The Ghost of Drag Racing's Past

By the close of the 1970 season, the SOHC 427 engine had seen its best days. With very few exceptions, all the fuel cars turned to running the more reliable Chrysler Hemi. One staunch believer in the old Cammer who refused to bow was Larry Gould. Larry continued to run the SOHC 427 long past its prime. He raced Al Bergler's old AA/FC Mustang II with Cammer power until 1982 when he replaced it with an EXP. He switched to an aftermarket Keith Black Hemi shortly thereafter.

Larry had a vast collection of Cammer engines and parts that kept him afloat. Like Pete Robinson years before, Larry fabricated several performance parts for the engine, including a gear drive to replace the troublesome chain that spun the cams. Around 2000, he built

Belleville, Illinois, resident Larry Gould did his best to make an SOHC 427 believer out of the masses when he ran that engine in his Mustang II. Reportedly, the car ran a best ET of 6.50. (Photo Courtesy Michael Pottie)

a Cammer-powered front-engine dragster that clocked a best 6.23 times. To this day, it is the quickest time ever turned by an SOHC 427.

Pro Stock

For the Mustang II, 1978 proved to be a dry year as no national event wins (NHRA, AHRA, or IHRA) were earned. The category was dominated by the Fairmont of Bob Glidden who refused to lose. Now, when it came to match racing, it was a whole different story.

The Marriott brothers purchased Scott Shafiroff's old Mustang II to replace their unique Shelby Pro Stocker. ETs for the Mustang II were in the 8.60s at 154 mph. (Photo Courtesy Dave Kommel)

Pro Stock's First 7-Second Pass

After the great year the Mustang II had in 1977, it's hard to believe that only one qualified at the 1978 NHRA season-opening Winternationals, and that was the car of Lee Hunter. Lee had purchased Bob Glidden's old Don Ness Mustang II from Jim Dowey and had won the Division 7 points championship with the car in 1976, after having won it in 1975 behind the wheel of a Pinto.

Lee's Mustang II was said to have made use of a 340-ci Cleveland, derived by boring out a sleeved 351 block and destroking it to 3.25. Lee's trip to the Winternationals ended early as he had the displeasure of meeting number-1 qualifier and eventual event winner Bob Glidden and his Pinto in the first round.

Dyno Don failed to make the Winternationals field after damaging his good engine. An engine transplant that dragged on saw him stuck in the staging lanes when qualifying ended.

Dyno's Mustang II racked up the miles, doubling down as a match racer and big-inch IHRA car. According a competitionplus.com interview with Dyno crewman Jon Kaase, Dyno went to a big-inch 516 engine at the beginning of the 1978 season. The engine was built upon an aluminum 429/460 block that was topped with aluminum heads that Ford produced in limited numbers in 1970. The bore measured 4.53 while a 4.00 stroke was created

A fresh coat of blue on Lee Hunter's Mustang II in 1977 was a vast improvement. Lee's Mustang ran an Earl Wade 340-ci Cleveland. Internals included a Crane camshaft and gear, Childs and Alberts rods, and Venolia gas-ported pistons. (Photo Courtesy Steve Reyes)

By 1978, Dyno Don's Mustang II was running 7-second match race times, thanks to a big-inch Wedge. Kaase, seen here holding steady, was compared favorably by Don to Earl Wade. The pair's working relationship ran through 1981. "PRO 1" on the window says it all. (Photo Courtesy Michael Pottie)

by turning down the journals from 2.50 to 2.20.

Horsepower for this torque monster was in the neighborhood of 900. It was on a Wednesday night in August that Don used the 516 to record Pro Stock's first 7-second pass. The historic moment came at a match race at Englishtown's Crazy Eddies Night of Thrills (later renamed Summer Motorsports Spectacular) when on a run against Grumpy Jenkins, Don recorded a 7.97 at 175 mph. The Mustang II was at a minimum weight of 1,900 pounds, thanks in part to the addition of lightweight windowless doors and a tall Formula 5000–style hood scoop to catch the good air.

It Gets Better:
Mountain Motors in the IHRA

When IHRA Competition Vice President Ted Jones was looking at ways to revamp Pro Stock in 1976, he turned to the exploding big-inch match races of

Week after week, Dyno Don match raced against competitors such as Grumpy Jenkins and Ronnie Sox. The championship Mustang ran a 516-ci Wedge while facing Jenkins here at Union Grove in May 1978. For match races, fiberglass doors replaced the class-legal steel parts. (Photo Courtesy Mike Sopko Sr.)

the South for inspiration. According to competitionplus.com, after viewing the racing down South, Jones told IHRA President Larry Carrier that they needed to come up with a new version of Pro Stock that got away from weight breaks. Ted presented Carrier with the minimal weight, maximum cubic-inch idea, which Jim jumped on, telling Tim, "Make it happen."

The new rules were implemented in 1977 and led to the first Mountain Motor Nationals in 1978. Held at Maryland International Raceway in August, the field was stacked with heavy hitters: Dyno in his 516-inch Mustang II, Ronnie Sox in the Sox & Martin Hemi Challenger, Lee Edwards's 490-inch Vega, Roy Hill in Pat Musi's Monza, Bob Glidden's Pinto, Larry Lombardo in Jenkins's Monza, and the Camaro of Bill Clayton.

The rules of the game were simple: any cubic inch, any weight, and no nitrous. As action got under way, both Edwards and Glidden fell with engine issues while Dyno, up next, broke his Lenco transmission. Roy Hill lost his doors in the lights while Sox headed back to the pits after his first burnout.

Bill Clayton was the first to make a full pass, opening up the action with an 8.56 at 159.23 mph. With repairs made to the broken cars, racing finally got under way.

Edwards lead with an 8.16 at 166.35 mph run, followed by Hill who turned an 8.20. Dyno was next with an 8.26 followed by Glidden's 8.27, Sox's 8.32, Lombardo's 8.32, Frank Iaconio's 8.41, and Clayton's 8.56. Round action saw the Fords of Dyno and Glidden eliminating the competition to face each other in the final. With Glidden having previously run a best of 8.27 and Dyno an 8.21, you knew it was going to be a close one.

Well, it should have been. The pair left side by side, but shortly out, Glidden's big-inch Cleveland went south, handing the win to Dyno, who recorded an 8.23 at 163.04.

Stocks and Super Stocks

NHRA rule changes now allowed the Super Stock cars to carry ballast, which those running Mustangs with their short deck really appreciated. Roll cages were now

John and Mary Jo Gass from Great Falls, Montana, were Winternational regulars with their SS/H 1969 convertible Crazy Horse II. The non–Ram Air Mustang was initially campaigned by Carl Holbrook before going to Brian Cour and then to John and Mary Jo. (Photo Courtesy Dave Kommel)

A consistent winner in Stock was the Southern California–based Crazy Horse of Richard Pickle. Richard partnered with George Blackwell and John Eckert, who usually drove the car. The Mustang was later sold to Steve Steele. (Photo Courtesy Dave Kommel)

The Winternationals just seemed to agree with Brian Cour. He won SS/FA class in 1973, SS/GA in 1975, and SS/F here in 1978. The same year, he also made four division final rounds. The Cour family continues to race today. (Photo Courtesy Dave Kommel)

required in SS/A to SS/DA cars and roll bars were required in cars SS/E through SS/K, and in convertibles down to SS/P.

It was another great season for the Mustangs of Stock and Super Stock with strong individual efforts grabbing headlines: John Turley from Sherman, Texas, and his CJ-powered 1969 Mustang knew no bounds, winning class in NHRA and IHRA competition.

The Ulrey brothers from Indiana continued with the wins they started back in the mid-1960s with an AA/S Galaxie by earning class honors (C and D/S) at the Springnationals with their pair of CJ Mustangs. Brian Cour seemed to have a thing for the Winternationals as he won his class for the third time in 1978, taking SS/F with his John Haskell–prepped 1968 Cobra Jet. National event wins made it a banner year for the Mustang.

Jeff Powers's Twin Wins

Jeff Powers ran a Norn Nevins CJ under the hood of his C/SA 1969 Mustang and won Stock Eliminator at both the NHRA Winternationals and the Cajun Nation-

Jeff Powers had quite the run, which included numerous class wins and records. In 1978, he won the Winternationals and the Cajun Nationals. In 1979, he was runner-up at the World Finals. Norm Nevin built the Cobra Jet for the Stocker. (Photo Courtesy Dave Kommel)

Mike Graham was another heavy hitter from the West Coast. Mike ran his Mustang as a 1971 and a 1972 model and held class records in G/S (12.03) and H/S (12.15) through a good part of 1978. The Mustang ran a best of 11.60s. (Photo Courtesy Dave Kommel)

als. Jeff, who last made a final round appearance in 1971 at the Supernationals, had done alright in between but never made another final-round appearance until 1978.

At the rain-soaked Winternationals, Jeff faced the Z/S Chevy Vega of George Williams to win the Eliminator. He missed out on the following Gatornationals but made up for it at the Cajun's in April, where he defeated the E/S Mercury of Gary Long in the final with an 11.73. Jeff and his Mustang set the class record in June with an 11.39 at 117.35 mph and carried it well into 1979.

Mike Graham

Mike Graham was another one of those who campaigned a 1971 Mustang as both a 1971 and a 1972 model. Appearance-wise the only difference between the two years was the gas cap. The 1971 used a pop-off cap and the 1972 used a screw-off cap. Mike ran the low-compression big-valve 351 with a 4-speed but did bolt up a C-6 to prove a point to his friend Joe Threatt.

It seems that Joe figured the only reason the Mustang was fast was because it was a 4-speed. Mike borrowed the C-6 out of Joe's own Mustang and proceeded to take the H/SA ET record away from him with a 12.31. Simultane-

ously, Mike also owned both ends of the H/S record with a 12.15 at 112.51 mph.

By using various combinations, Mike could run G through I/Stock and was capable of setting the record in each. Mike was a proven engine builder and professes that there was nothing trick about his combination.

"[I] paid close attention to specs, ring combinations, and valve springs," he said.

Behind the Cleveland, Mike ran a GER transmission with its straight-cut gears (like Jerico makes today).

GER was the first with the design, and Jim's Mustang was the test car.

"We had transmissions and gear ratios that very few people had, although they weren't the most reliable as they didn't know how to heat-treat," he said.

Back when everyone else was using a 2.78 or 2.87 low gear, Jim was able to run a 3.29 low gear. Filling the rear were gears ranging from 5.14 to 5.43. Suspension modifications were limited to traction bars and modified shocks. Mike raced the Mustang from 1976 through 1981 before Jim Meyers took over behind the wheel and won Stock Eliminator with it at the 1982 NHRA Winternationals. The Mustang was sold shortly after.

With S. E. Buchanan behind the wheel, the team of Kuntz & Buchanan cleaned house in 1977, winning class at multiple events, setting the class record, and winning their division. (Photo Courtesy Dave Kommel)

Kuntz & Buchanan

Heading east to Arkansas, the home of the fried pickle and chocolate gravy, was the much-feared team of S. E. Buchanan and Jim Kuntz. The pair used their 1969 Mach 1 to win its third of four in a row Division 4 championships in 1978. The two joined forces in late 1975 and became one of the most feared teams in Stock class drag racing.

By 1975, Jim had already earned the reputation as one of the nation's top engine builders, while S. E., a drag racer going back to the early 1960s when he raced the Arkansas I-30 drag strip, was better than most on the tree. S .E. was a likeable person, known as a racer's racer, and gladly gave a hand to fellow competitors at the track.

The pair's biggest win of 1978 came at the Sportsnationals, where S. E. won the event after playing runner-up in 1977. The team ran the Mustang in both C/S and D/S

After a brief hiatus, the team of Kuntz & Buchanan returned in 1982 with this convertible to win class at Indy. (Photo Courtesy Brian Buchanan)

to earn additional points and held the D/S record for a good part of the season with an 11.45 at 117.64 mph. After campaigning a borrowed A/SM Mustang in the early 1980s, Kuntz & Buchanan returned in 1982 with a D/S 1969 Mustang convertible powered by a Cobra Jet to win the U.S. Nationals.

EPILOGUE

Like father like son. Chris Holbrook learned a lot from his father, Carl, and continued on his winning ways. Today, Chris heads Holbrook Performance engines out of Chattanooga, Tennessee. (Photo Courtesy Dan Williams)

As the following decades have shown us, the on-track heroics of the Mustang didn't end with the 1970s. With the Mustang's 60th anniversary creeping up on us, the car's on-track success shows no sign of ebbing. It continues to be a winner in multiple classes and categories.

As of this writing, the 1968–1970 CJ cars continue to be a threat in Stock and Super Stock. It's safe to say that they always will be. There's little doubt that these cars have been Ford's most successful on-track representative. In recent years, they have faced a challenge to the throne by way of the

This shot of Tracy Miller's CJ Mustang was taken in 1988. Tracy's success proved that the apple doesn't fall far from the tree. Her father, Aldon, a Stock Eliminator star of the Northwest, bought this Mustang new. (Photo Courtesy Larry Pfister)

Harold Denton purchased this Fox Body terror from Dyno Don in 1981. The 580-plus-ci Boss was good for 7.80 times. Harold was voted number 17 on the list of top IHRA Mountain Motor Pro Stock racers. (Photo Courtesy Jim Kampmann)

Factory Stock Cobra Jet Mustangs. Today, these cars threaten the popularity of the Pro Stock category.

Pro Stock (tired of the ridiculous weight breaks that hampered the Fords through the 1970s) was set on its ear when the IHRA introduced new rules to the game in 1977. It did away with the weight breaks and went to a minimum 2,350-pound weight, and a no-limit cubic-inch format. The party was on. In short order, you had Fox Body Mustangs dipping well into the 7s. Dyno Don, Rickie Smith, and Dean Thompson all made record holders and world champs out of the Fox Body Mustang.

The NHRA, following the lead of the IHRA, adopted similar rules in 1982, going with a 2,350-pound minimum but a 500-ci maximum. Today, you could say the NHRA has lost the objective. Rules have changed so drastically that the category has become a one-car show. You need to go back at least five years to find anything other than

a Camaro in the winner's circle. The NHRA has gotten so desperate for any other brand to win that it now allows any brand of engine in any brand of car. Talk about killing the category. Is it any wonder why the Factory Stock cars have become so popular?

Factory Stock is similar in concept to the ideals of Pro Stock as it originated: a heads-up category with minimal rules and maximum performance. Factory Stock is limited to COPO Camaros, Drag Pak Challengers, and Cobra Jet Mustangs. The NHRA refers to its program as Factory Stock Showdown while the National Muscle Car Association runs a similar program referred to as Factory Super Cars.

The class of cars took off around 2014, but Ford got an early jump in 2008, when it produced the Mustang Cobra Jet, which was a factory-built drag car. It was built to celebrate the 40th anni-

Today, Factory Stock is the hot ticket. Here, at Indy in 2019, Bo Butner goes wheels-up against Bill Skillman on another mid-7-second blast. Skillman's 2014 Mustang won this event, defeating the 2019 Camaro of Arthur Kohn. (Photo Courtesy Dan Williams)

versary of the Mustang's original release. Today, the supercharged Mustangs of Factory Stock are clocking mid-7-second times with stock bodies and 9-inch slicks.

Who knows what drag racing's future will hold. In 2021, the NHRA introduced an electric vehicle class. To compete, Ford has an E-Cobra Jet 1400 Mustang in the wings that produces 1,400 hp and 1,100 pounds of torque. The future is now, and it appears that the Mustang may once again lead the charge. Stay tuned.

Additional books that may interest you...

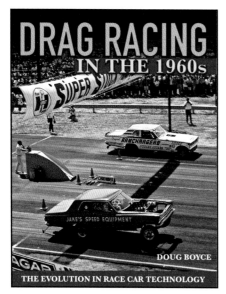

DRAG RACING IN THE 1960s:
The Evolution in Race Car Technology
by Doug Boyce
In this book veteran author Doug Boyce takes you on a ride through the entire decade from a technological point of view rather than a results-based one. 8.5 x 11", 176 pgs, 350 photos, Sftbd. ISBN 9781613255827 Part # CT674

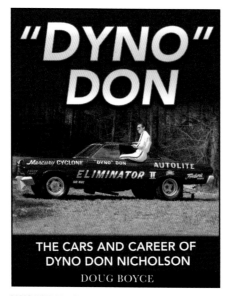

DYNO DON: The Cars and Career of Dyno Don Nicholson *by Doug Boyce*
If you are a fan of a certain era of racing, a Ford fan, or certainly a "Dyno Don" fan this book will be a welcome addition to your library. Follow his Hall of Fame career on the match race circuit. 8.5 x 11", 176 pgs, 330 photos, Sftbd. ISBN 9781613254059 Part # CT631

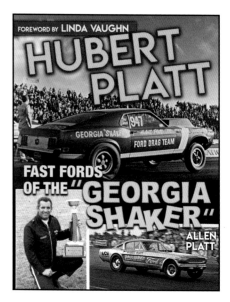

HUBERT PLATT: Fast Fords of the "Georgia Shaker" *by Allen Platt*
Hubert Platt's son Allen presents this chronological history of Hubert's racing career. Included are never-before-seen, personal photos from the Platt Family Collection accompanied by records and documents showcasing Platt's illustrious drag-racing career. 8.5 x 11", 192 pgs, 427 photos, Sftbd. ISBN 9781613253977 Part # CT625

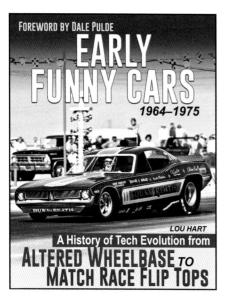

EARLY FUNNY CARS: A History of Tech Evolution from Altered Wheelbase to Match Race Flip Tops 1964–1975 *by Lou Hart*
Blast through the evolving early years of Funny Car drag racing when doorslammers morphed into flip-top rail monsters. The era features historic mounts from Arnie "the Farmer" Beswick, Al "the Flying Dutchman" Vanderwoude, "Jungle" Jim Liberman, Don "the Snake" Prudhomme, and many more! .8.5 x 11" Part # CT683

Check out our website:

CarTechBooks.com

✓ **Find our newest books before anyone else**

✓ **Get weekly tech tips from our experts**

✓ **Featuring a new deal each week!**

Exclusive Promotions and Giveaways at www.CarTechBooks.com!

www.cartechbooks.com or
1-800-551-4754

Get the latest from CarTech on facebook!